UNIVERSITY OF SOUTHERN CALIFORNIA
STUDIES IN COMPARATIVE LITERATURE
Volume V

THE
FRONTIERS
OF
LITERARY
CRITICISM

Edited
and with an introduction
by

David H. Malone

HENNESSEY & INGALLS, INC.
Los Angeles   1974

Acknowledgment

Lothar Stiehm Verlag, GMBH, Heidelberg. For permission to reprint from their *Der Dichter und seine Zeit* (1970) the English version of the article by Peter Demetz, "Transformations of Recent Marxist Criticism: Hans Mayer, Ernst Fischer, Lucien Goldmann."

801.95
F 92
97576
July 1976

Library of Congress Cataloging in Publication Data

Main entry under title:
Frontiers of literary criticism.

(University of Southern California studies in comparative literature, 5)

Consists of essays based on papers presented at the Third Conference on Comparative Literature, held at the University of Southern California, Apr. 24-25, 1969.

1. Criticism—Adresses, essays, lectures.
I. Malone, David H., 1919-   ed. II. Series: Los Angeles. University of Southern California. Studies in comparative literature, 5.

PN94.F7   801'.95   76-188988

Clothbound ISBN 0-912158-19-0
Paperbound ISBN 0-912158-56-5

CONTENTS

PREFACE

The essays which appear in this volume were originally presented as papers at the Third Conference on Comparative Literature held on the campus of the University of Southern California on April 24 and 25, 1969. The principal participants in the Conference were invited to prepare presentations under the general topic of "The Frontiers of Literary Criticism." The essays which appear in this volume in some cases represent essentially the same texts presented orally at the Conference, and in other cases modified or expanded versions of the original texts.

Unfortunately, this volume does not constitute the "Proceedings" of the Third Conference on Comparative Literature, but only the principal papers upon which the discussions of the Conference were based. As stimulating as the essays reproduced here may be, the discussions of the original papers were often even more stimulating and undoubtedly contributed materially to revisions made by some of the authors. It seems appropriate, therefore, to express appreciation to the formal discussants, whose contributions to the Third Comparative Literature Conference were obvious and significant, but whose contributions to this volume,

1

although indirect and submerged, are also important: Ann Stanford, California State University at Northridge; Ralph Freedman, Princeton University; John Fuegi, University of Wisconsin at Milwaukee; Egon Schwarz, Washington University; Peter Clothier, University of Southern California; Richard Hutson, University of California at Berkeley; Lawrence L. Stahlberger, Stanford University; and Rainer Vadim Grenewitz, University of California at Irvine.

Both this volume and the Conference on Comparative Literature upon which it is based have been made possible only through the generous support of the Graduate School of the University of Southern California. Both to Milton C. Kloetzel, Vice President for Academic Affairs, and to Charles G. Mayo, Dean of the Graduate School, I want to express the deep appreciation of myself and my colleagues on the faculty of the University of Southern California and on the Editorial Board of the USC *Studies in Comparative Literature* for their enthusiastic encouragement and support.

It was originally planned that this volume would appear in 1970, but as in all scholarly ventures involving a number of people, unexpected delays in the preparation of the manuscript compounded problems already confronting the publisher so that this collection appears later than we had hoped. Although the authors represented in this volume might well wish to have modified a few things in their essays in the light of recent developments in criticism, the nine essays remain a significant collection of forays along The Frontiers of Literary Criticism.

D. H. M.

Los Angeles
July, 1973

INTRODUCTION

David H. Malone

It has been well over a third of a century since New Criticism effected a revolution in the teaching of literature in the United States, and therefore in literary studies and literary criticism itself. Some of us can still recall that just as the victory of New Criticism over the forces of historical scholarship was being announced, many proclaimed our age, if not our century, the Age of Criticism. One may ask just what an "Age of Criticism" is, but probably one indication lies in the amount of informed, literate, and useful criticism being written. If sheer quantity of critical writing is the principal means of defining an Age of Criticism, then it seems even more apparent today than it did on the eve of the triumph of New Criticism that the twentieth century is indeed an Age of Criticism. But while the quantity of critical writing remains today perhaps even greater than it was a quarter of a century ago, the nature, purpose, and tone of critical writing today is vastly different from that of the "New Critics"—however different they may have been among themselves.

During the battles over New Criticism it was easy, if not

necessary, to take sides, to know which side of the battle one favored. On the one side were those who insisted upon scholarship, indeed who preferred to be called scholars rather than critics, who published in such journals as *PMLA, Studies in Philology,* or the *Journal of English and Germanic Philology.* On the other side were those who proudly called themselves critics, who regarded scholarship as little more than the menial, if necessary preparation for the important work of criticism itself, and who published in such journals as the *Kenyon Review,* the *Southern Review,* or the *Hudson Review.* The "critics" were for the most part outside the academic establishment—that is, they rarely had tenure on university faculties and certainly numbered few if any department chairmen of English departments among them.

Things have changed. Today any critic will boast of the impeccability of his scholarship, and every scholar insists that whatever he does is an act of literary criticism. Things have not changed so much that articles in *PMLA* and the *Kenyon Review* are entirely indistinguishable from one another, but every now and then one finds an article in either journal which the other might have printed. Tenure faculties and department chairmen today are usually far more impressed by a young applicant's record of publication in what might be thought of as criticism than by a record consisting of textual or bibliographical or historical study, however important and meticulous it might be.

It is probably another instance of the victors writing both law and history and even, to a certain extent, being taken over by those whom they conquered. For today criticism readily encompasses and utilizes the historical, sociological, biographical, and economic approaches to literary study which seemed anathema to the pure New Critic. But if the victory of New Criticism over a third of a century ago ushered in the Age of Criticism, that "Age" today seems far different from the one of New Criticism. New Criticism was a peculiarly, almost parochially, Anglo-American development, both in the academic and geographic senses. It was only later, by means of a kind of fall-out from the explosions of New Criticism, that significant modifications were made in the way literature was taught in foreign language departments. And the influence of New Criticism on the European Continent was hardly commensurate with the uproar in North America.

Today's criticism encompasses activities, research, reciprocal influences that include not only all of the humanistic disciplines but most other fields of knowledge as well. Furthermore, the exchange of ideas, insights, and strategies between scholar-critics on the European and American continents is probably the most stimulating and productive feature of contemporary criticism. If the main issues in the critical disputes of twenty-five and thirty-five years ago were clear— at least, if with hindsight we can see where criticism was going—what in our "Age of Criticism" is all of the critical activity about? Is the great variety of stimulating, prolific, far-ranging critical writing that is being done today an indication that we are indeed engaged in something of historical or even educational importance? It is difficult right now to know, and certainly impossible to be sure. In his recent book, *Synthetisches Interpretieren* (1968), Jost Hermand finds so much chaos in the variety of critical activities and disputes that he wonders if we might not find peace and unity once more in a new form of historical criticism.

> Wohin man auch hört, schallen einem neue Schlagworte entgegen: Literatursoziologie, Motivgeschichte, Psychoanalyse, Marxismus, Generationstheorie, Geistesswissenschaft, New Criticism, Kunst der Interpretation, immanente Werkanalyse, Gattungsgeschichte, wechselseitige Erhellung der Kunste, morphologische Literaturwissenschaft, Existentialismus, Problemgeschichte, Strukturalismus, Literaturbiologie, Phanomenologie,

David H. Malone

linguistische Methode, oder reiner Formalismus. Was
soll uns da noch ein neuer "Ismus"? Haben wir nicht
genug an dem, was wir bereits besitzen? (p. 7)

And indeed since the triumph of New Criticism the variety of
new critical approaches that have been explored is bewildering. Wellek and Warren in their *Theory of Literature* were
able to map out clearly defined paths for future criticism to
follow, but even those who followed those paths find themselves today faced with such a multiplicity of possibilities
that they are almost forced into some kind of superficial
eclecticism, into a militant dogmatism, or into an earnest,
difficult, and probably forever elusive search for a new path
that will enable a reader to articulate the significance of his
confrontation with a work of literature or of that work of
literature itself.

Professor Hermand seems to have felt in his fine book that
the only way out of the bewildering confusion of contemporary criticism was to return to a form of historical criticism. The academic sensibility finds security in history.
History is there—in the past—and it changes only if we make
unexpected new discoveries of what we hadn't known was
there. But however effectively we may be able to read and
study literature as a part of history, as a function of history,
even as a part of our present in the sense that all of the past is
part of the present, the question of what our society will do
with literature in the future remains. It is by no means
inevitable that literature will remain an essential part of the
education of future generations. If the question of the future
of literature in Western society, even in the future of education, is to be answered, it will not be answered by historical
criticism, but rather by those who are struggling on what we
have chosen to call, for the purpose of assembling the discussions contained in this volume, the "frontiers of literary
criticism."

In a great variety of voices, languages, traditions, and

strategies, a large number of critics today are addressing themselves to the truly important questions about literature in our culture. Will all of this activity have anything like the significant implications for teaching and literary study that the work of the New Critics of the late thirties and forties had in the English-speaking world? Is ours simply an era of pluralistic criticism in which every critical strategy is just as legitimate as every other? Has criticism in its intricate relationship to the academic establishment—especially in America—become little more than an arcane game by means of which the practitioners advance themselves within an academic bureaucracy? Or perhaps we should go back to a question with which we should have begun: the question that has always been asked about criticism, and therefore about literature. Does all of this critical activity in our "Age of Criticism" really reveal more to us about what a work of literary art is, how it comes into being, how it works, and what its value to the human race is? Because ours is, if not an "Age of Criticism," certainly an age in which a very great deal of criticism is being written, it seemed appropriate to undertake a symposium on the topic, "The Frontiers of Literary Criticism."

To be sure, there is something almost inevitably pejorative in the term "Frontiers of Criticism," as Donald Davie suggests at the end of his discussion in this volume. The term itself suggests what has, in every age, been said about critics, that they take themselves and their activities more seriously than they are worth. It even suggests, almost invidiously, that in our age criticism can make new "discoveries" analogous to those made in the natural sciences. Whatever the disadvantages of the term, however, it does suggest the questions which need to be asked about the role and study of literature in our society and it does imply something of the importance of the work that the contributors to this volume are doing.

Certainly René Wellek's "A Map of Contemporary Criticism in Europe" and Victor Lange's "Perspectives of Contemporary German Criticism" confirm the amount, variety, and originality of critical activity going on in our age. Mr. Davie's "British Criticism: The Necessity for Humility" suggests that much of this activity is too self-conscious, too frenzied, and—while he does not say it, he certainly implies it—too arrogant. On the other hand, Ihab Hassan's experiment in paracriticism, entitled "Frontiers of Criticism: Metaphors of Silence," dramatizes in and of itself the kind of crisis implied in our term "Frontier." It just could be, he seems to suggest, that the whole tradition of discursive criticism is now bankrupt, and that whatever we do to explore, communicate, or understand the mystery involved in the experience of a work of art must hereafter involve at least something other than discursive analysis.

Despite the almost apocalyptic perspective on the current status of literary criticism represented by Mr. Hassan's experiment in paracriticism, one of the most interesting aspects of the current welter of critical activity is that nothing *genuinely* new seems to be developing, but new and exciting utilizations of critical approaches of the past promise new insights into the nature and function of literature. Peter Demetz finds significance in the work of such younger Marxist critics as Hans Mayer, Lucien Goldmann, and especially Ernst Fischer, even though he feels they are still too inhibited by Marxist historicism. Michael Riffaterre's review of "French Formalism" might suggest to the superficial reader that France is only now getting around to the battle between the New Critics and the establishmentarian historical scholars. But the significance of what has happened in the development of French Formalist Criticism lies in no way in any kind of spurious analogues of New Criticism, but in the way the earnest quest to define the formal structure of a work of literature has compelled the French critic, despite himself, beyond the text, or at least to look upon the literary text as just one of the many kinds of "texts" by means of which man seeks to represent the "reality" of his world.

Thus, for all of the pressures of the formalist approach to make the work of literature a self-contained ontological entity, the French critics are exploring quite new ways of defining and exploring the mimetic component of literature, and this exploration has compelled them to make new and fresh uses of developments in linguistics, anthropology, psychology, sociology, and so on. The fascinating practical possibilities of these explorations are illustrated in René Girard's original and penetrating reading of Shakespeare's *A Midsummer Night's Dream,* in which his search for, what one might call, the "deep structure" underlying Shakespeare's play reveals the play to be anything but a self-contained ontological entity, but rather a particular kind of mimetic representation of reality that demonstrates the play to be profoundly more revealing and universal than any traditional readings have suggested.

Even as new approaches to the understanding of literature may be developing by re-examinations of Marxist critical theory, extensions of Russian Formalism, refinements of traditional textual analysis, and so on, Edward Wasiolek seeks, in his "The Future of Psychoanalytic Criticism," to rescue such criticism from the sloppiness of its earliest practitioners and from the simplistic schema and jargon derived from Freud. Indeed, Mr. Wasiolek implies that one of the most significant frontiers for literary criticism lies in the refinement of psychoanalytic techniques and their fusion with techniques developed by the formalists and structuralists, whether of America or France.

While the emphasis in this volume is upon the critical ferment of Western Europe and the United States, Edward J. Brown, in his "Some New Directions in Russian Literary Criticism," demonstrates that comparable activity has been taking place in the Soviet Union. The most striking development in Soviet criticism, at least up until a new ice age seemed to begin moving across the thawing intellectual climate of the late fifties and early sixties, has been the intense interaction between literature and other disciplines. Mr. Brown outlines in particular some of the contributions to literary criticism from such diverse areas as the natural sciences, mathematics, cybernetics, cinema, and even from new approaches to the study of traditional literature. The fact that Soviet critics and scholars have within the last decade suddenly become interested in Comparative Literature (even to the point of having sent sizable delegations to the last two Congresses of the International Comparative Literature Association) holds out the promise both that Western criticism may benefit immensely from new approaches developed by Soviet critics, and that Soviet criticism may in time explore and refine some of the ideas and techniques being developed in the West.

There is no pretense, even as there was no intention, that this volume should represent all of the activities that might be taking place on the "frontiers of literary criticism." What the essays in this volume do convincingly demonstrate is that a great deal and variety of intensely intelligent, imaginative, promising, and stimulating literary criticism is being written today. It may well be that much of it is pompous, self-important, remote from the actual experience of reading a work of literature. But it seems more likely, from the evidence contained in these essays, that critics are pushing through and past literature to discover how every activity of the human being is, directly or indirectly, absorbed in the individual work of literary art. It may be that literary critics are really beginning to work on the "frontiers of knowledge" in other disciplines and will in time discover the means through literary criticism of restoring literature to its traditionally central role in human life and human culture.

UNIVERSITY OF SOUTHERN CALIFORNIA

A MAP OF CONTEMPORARY CRITICISM IN EUROPE

René Wellek

For many years I have been engaged in writing a *History of Modern Criticism* from the middle of the eighteenth century to the present. Four volumes were published, two in 1955 and two in 1965 taking down the story to about 1900. A last volume on the twentieth century is still unfinished. Obviously it is a more difficult task to write about the twentieth century than on the eighteenth or nineteenth centuries as there is no book such as Saintsbury's *History of Criticism and Literary Taste in Europe* (published between 1901 and 1904) which would even give an outline of the subject. There are, of course, some books and articles on developments in individual countries, but even those are not plentiful and not up to date, for the most part. Still, from the perspective of 1968 it is fairly clear who are the outstanding figures in literary criticism in the early decades of this century: we can hardly hesitate in naming Benedetto Croce in Italy, Albert Thibaudet, Charles Du Bos, and Paul Valéry in France, T. S. Eliot, I. A. Richards, and F. R. Leavis in England and, at least to a Western observer, Georg Lukács will appear as the most

11

prominent Marxist critic in the East. We may have doubts about whom we should single out in Germany. Germany in the early part of the century produced a distinguished group of scholar-critics: Friedrich Gundolf, who belonged to the circle around Stefan George; and four great experts in the Romance literatures: Karl Vossler, Ernst Robert Curtius, Leo Spitzer, and Erich Auerbach of whom the last two emigrated late in their lives to the United States. But there was no great public figure comparable to those I mentioned in the other countries. Possibly Walter Benjamin could, in retrospect, assume such stature. But he was isolated and desperately alone in his time. Ortega y Gasset seems easily the most conspicuous figure in Spain.

If we want to know the state of criticism at the present moment—and such knowledge seems to be indispensable even to a historian of the remote past—our uncertainty grows, the selection of the major figures becomes controversial, as the discord of voices and clash of opinions grows louder and more raucous. The picture in one's mind vacillates and shifts disconcertingly and seems to change almost every year. It would be, I imagine, possible to sit down in a well-stocked library and read as much as one can to form an opinion about the present situation in every country. But this seems not enough. No doubt, one has to know the books and read the periodicals but besides, I think, there is a need to acquire through personal contacts some sense of the atmosphere, the lay of the land, the relative importance of people, books, and issues. I traveled in Europe repeatedly and extensively in recent years meeting with critics and literary scholars; not interviewing them in any formal manner (I detest tape re-corders) but talking freely and frankly. I hope I have thus acquired a knowledge of what I like to call the geography or map of contemporary European criticism.

In the space at my disposal here I cannot provide more than a brief Cook's tour of the main countries which might give you some feeling of the enormous activity in criticism in Europe today. I hope to arouse your curiosity which can, at least, in part be satisfied by reading and I hope to make you reflect on one overwhelming impression I carried away from my travels: the sense of the gulfs that are yawning between the different national traditions in spite of all the many attempts at building bridges: a sense of the tenacity with which the main European nations cling to their distant critical traditions and even within one nation, a sense of the almost equally unbridgeable chasms that divide schools, ideologies, and individuals. One comes away sometimes disheartened by a sense of the worse than Babylonian confusion of tongues that afflicts criticism possibly more than any other comparable human activity. It is often very difficult to understand the terminology and assumptions of much foreign criticism if one starts with any kind of preconceptions and a vocabulary of one's own as one inevitably does. It requires acts of mental acrobatics or put more modestly, acts of surrender of one's individuality, to enter into the minds of so diverse men starting from premises which are strikingly different from my own. Fortunately I am not entirely unprepared, as my own experience was varied enough during my early life in Europe, largely in Czechoslovakia and England.

England is the country which for obvious reasons is best known to Americans. The links in criticism have been particularly strong in this century: two Americans who settled in England: Ezra Pound and T. S. Eliot were enormously influential also as critics, and an Englishman, I. A. Richards, who moved from Cambridge on the Cam to Cambridge on the Charles River can be considered the father of the American New Criticism. He was also the teacher of William Empson and he, together with Eliot, greatly influenced the early development of F. R. Leavis who is still a dominant force in English criticism.

The many pupils and adherents of Leavis have been extremely active. Older men such as L. C. Knights who earned his spurs with the famous attack on A. C. Bradley: *How Many Children Had Lady Macbeth?* (1933) has more recently written on *Some Shakespearean Themes* (1959) and *An Approach to Hamlet* (1960). Derek Traversi, a Welshman in spite of his Italian name, is another Leavisite: *Shakespeare: The Last Phase* (1955) is a recent book of his; and Martin Turnell, *Scrutiny's* French specialist, has produced a steady stream of books on *The Novel in France* (1951), on *Baudelaire* (1953), and *The Art of French Fiction* (1959). The widely sold and used *Pelican Guide to English Literature* is almost entirely written by Leavis pupils in his spirit. John Holloway, in a section of the last volume, proclaims the writings of F. R. Leavis "the outstanding critical achievement of the century in English" (p. 90). John Holloway himself, who has made his name by a good book *The Victorian Sage,* dismisses all philosophical and aesthetic speculation as "abracadabra" in the good anti-theoretical manner of Leavis, and argues at length against the American New Criticism and its cult of complexity, paradox, and irony as well as against the Chicago Aristotelianism and the ambiguities of William Empson. What remains is an Arnoldian "calm intelligence," "moderation," and "urbanity" and his insights into the implications of life and literature as the ideal of criticism.

W. W. Robson, who is one of the editors of the *Cambridge Quarterly,* is even closer to Leavis's point of view. His *Critical Essays* show the same concern for the moral life in literature, for the central role of English studies as a discipline of sensibility and the somewhat surprising exaltation of D. H. Lawrence both as a novelist and critic. Robson, in a recent lecture, defended "criticism without principles." Literary criticism is neither a science nor a mass of fancies but a personal encounter with the great works. "There is no body of established results which the next critic can build on" (*Critical Essays,* p. 34). There is not even a continuous debate.

The very same point of view is upheld by George Watson, in *The Literary Critics* (1962). He is, in general, not well-disposed toward Leavis—he feels that Leavis has "hurried towards value-judgments without respect to the essential delicacy and complexity of literary values" (p. 215). But Watson himself dismisses all theory and all evaluation and recognizes only "descriptive" criticism denying "continuity and intelligibility in the history of literary argument." He sees in criticism only "a record of chaos marked by sudden revolution." He concludes strikingly, "The great critics do not contribute; they interrupt." For quite mysterious reasons an "anticognitive enthusiasm" is attributed to me (p. 221), possibly because I have argued against the excesses of historicism.

Historicism is quite comprehensibly the creed of many academic critics in England as elsewhere. Helen Gardner's *The Business of Criticism* (1960) is an eloquent statement and a defense of "intention" as the legitimate and ultimate aim of the critic's quest.

But most practicing critics show rather a contemporary social concern. It dominates the books of Raymond Williams who criticizes Leavis's assumption of a "wholly organic and satisfying past" and advocates a democratic socialism. In *Culture and Society, 1780-1950* he shares, however, Leavis's main worry about the triumphs of a technological civilization destroying the old tradition of humanist culture.

Frank Kermode, in his *Romantic Image* (1957), made a powerful attack on the whole conception of poetry as imagery and symbol. He sees the idea that Image is "radiant truth out of space and time" as "a great and in some ways noxious historical myth" (p. 166) which, he argues, entails the equally false myth of the necessary isolation and estrangement of the modern artist. Kermode, though he admired Yeats as the culmination of this tradition, wishes its demise. He advocates, surprisingly, a return to Milton. In his newest book, *Continuities* (1968), he thinks of himself as a new Edmund Wilson: a social critic who, however, preserves a proper grasp on the nature of art. Kermode becomes quite satirical about the new *avant-garde,* about pop and op art, the music of silence, etc., where "the difference between art and joke is as obscure as that between art and non-art" (p. 15).

Theoretical reflections on the problems of criticism have come recently from philosophers or rather the adherents of analytical philosophy deeply impressed by Wittgenstein's criticism of language. John Casey's *The Language of Criticism* (1966) avoids the sterile dismissal of all questions of aesthetics and valuation, which is also the trite conclusion of most descriptive linguists who try with statistical and quantitative methods to impose criteria of scientific objectivity on the study of literature. Casey sees, to my mind correctly, that "in aesthetics the concept of a personal 'response' is central, while we must at the same time avoid the view which is often taken to be a corollary of that—that aesthetic judgment is ultimately 'subjective.' " But Casey moves on a high level of abstraction remote from actual literary criticism while the linguists are rather concerned with "taking a poem to pieces," with minute observations on syntax, grammar, and meter. Two books, Christine Brooke-Rose's *A Grammar of Metaphor* (1958), technical and scholastic as it is, and Winifred Nowottny's *The Language Poets Use* (1962), raise problems of criticism as does David Lodge's *Language of Fiction* (1966) which offers more than a "Verbal Analysis of the English Novel" promised in the title. It bridges the usual gulf between linguistic analysis and interpretive and evaluative criticism very successfully. These recent books contradict the ingrained anti-theoretical prejudice of the English strikingly formulated by H. W. Garrod, Professor of Poetry at Oxford, when he said that "criticism is best when written with the least worry of head, the least disposition to break the heart over ultimate questions."

This is precisely what the French are doing. If we cross the Channel we must be struck by the violent clash of theories and ideologies. There is a new Marxism very much alive (while dead in England since the thirties), sophisticated, sharply aware of Hegel and Lukács of which Lucien Goldmann may be singled out as the best representative. His book on Pascal and Racine, *Le Dieu caché*, showed how tragedy and tragic vision can be linked with social changes and social groups ("la noblesse de robe") in ways which nobody could have thought of before. There is a flourishing interest in psychoanalysis, Freudian and Jungian in France. Charles Mauron who died late in 1966 aroused even academic respect by his studies of Mallarmé and obsessive metaphors. A philosopher of science, Gaston Bachelard produced a psychoanlysis of fire and followed it up, not unexpectedly, with books on air, earth, and water.

But the most flourishing and original movement in French criticism calls itself "la critique de conscience." The group, sometimes referred to also as the Geneva school, reveres Marcel Raymond for his book *Du Baudelaire au Surréalisme* (1933) as the originator of the method but actually went far beyond him in formulating a new way of studying literature. They aim not at an analysis or judgment of a single work of literature but rather at a reconstruction of the peculiar consciousness of a writer. Every poet is assumed to have lived or to live in his peculiar world which has an interior organization or "structure" which it is the task of the critic to discover and articulate. The emphasis on various aspects differs from critic to critic. Georges Poulet is primarily interested in the attitude to time of poets and writers which he traced in several books (*Etudes sur le temps humain*, 1950; *La Distance intérieur*, 1952) with unparalleled ingenuity. In recent publications, particularly *Les Métamorphoses du cercle* (1961), Poulet has moved toward generalizations about Renaissance, Baroque, and Romanticism. Consciousness is an all-embracing spirit of the time. Romanticism, for instance, is described as an effort to overcome the opposition of subject and object, of center and circumference, in a personal experience. Jean Pierre Richard, a much younger man, is concerned rather with analyzing the perceptual life of the authors he discusses. We hear, e.g., that for Flaubert love is like drowning or that the lover loses his bones, becomes like plastic paste. *Littérature et sensation* (1954) is the apt title of his first book. Sentences and observations, metaphors and scenes from all books, diaries, letters, and jottings of an author are used, without regard to context in order to build up a scheme of his mental life or of the imaginary universe of a poet such as Mallarmé, organized by leading motifs, obsessive metaphors, or recurrent stylistic devices. Richard's perspective is resolutely anti-formal. He considers his approach superior to what he calls "Anglo-Saxon criticism" as it does not consider external form and linguistic surface but establishes "a connection, an immediately felt echo between the forms of its expression (syntactic, rhetorical, melodic) and the shapes (thematic or ideological) of the deep experience it expresses and incarnates" (Preface to *Onze Etudes,* pp. 9-10). In Richard literature is conceived as an imaginary universe in which individual problems or "projects" move toward their solutions.

Another member of the Geneva group Jean Starobinski is very close to Richard in theory though in his interests he differs by a stress on the Enlightenment and its "invention of freedom." His book on Rousseau (1957) is actually a psychological study which describes Rousseau as searching for "transparency," for a communion of human hearts and when rebuffed erecting a subjective "obstacle" within himself. Language, as in Bishop Berkeley, is conceived of as an impediment to direct vision because it throws a "veil" over reality. Raymond's successor, Jean Rousset, is much more interested in form and has tried in his books on the Baroque in France and in *Forme et signification* (1962) to build bridges between the existential criticism of his training and a grasp of literature as art. The living organism, the "focus" of a work of art are terms which are to connect the two sides: form and meaning. Among the so-called "critics of conscience" Albert Béguin and Maurice Blanchot stand somewhat apart. Béguin, who had written an excellent book on *L'Ame romantique et le rêve* (1939) which studies German Romanticism and the French writers who followed in the exaltation of the life of dreams: Baudelaire, Rimbaud, Mallarmé, and Proust, turned in his later writings to Catholic mysticism. Maurice Blanchot, a most difficult and even obscure writer, discusses in *L'Espace littéraire* (1955) such questions as "whether literature is possible?" or the "space of death" using Kafka, Mallarmé and Hölderlin as examples. Blanchot arrives at a strange nihilism: silence is the ultimate significance of literature. The ineffable is the only thing left to express. Fortunately, there are more articulate and rational critics in France.

Poulet, Richard, Blanchot are sometimes referred to as structuralists but their structuralism has nothing to do with what the term means to linguists and literary theorists who have always used it as referring to the structure or pattern of a language or a work of art. Roland Barthes appeals to the linguistic and anthropological concept of structure and speculates about an all-inclusive theory of signs which he has illustrated by a study of feminine fashions. But his little book on *Racine* (1963) draws rather on Freudian psychoanalysis and a Jungian concept of archetypal myth than on linguistics. The situation of every drama of Racine is reduced to an equation: "A has complete power over B. A loves B, who does not love A." A kind of abstract thematology emerges enlivened by references to solar myth, oedipal relations, and a parallel in historical events. No wonder that he was violently attacked by an exponent of the historical method, Raymond Picard. Barthes defended himself, in *Critique et vérité* (1966), pleading for an almost complete freedom of symbolic interpretation for what seems, in practice, an arbitrary "creative" criticism duplicating the work of art.

In general, what is called today "structuralism" in France and has attracted much public attention through the success of the work in anthropology of Claude Lévi-Strauss is a bafflingly diverse and even contradictory set of doctrines with the most diverse philosophical affiliations: the mood of Sartre's existentialism, the techniques of Husserl's phenomenology, the fanciful pseudo-science of Gaston Bachelard, modern linguists ultimately derived from de Saussure, and sometimes, Marxism or Marxist motifs. It provides a rich hodgepodge of methods which—whatever the interest and stimulation afforded may be—suffers to my mind from the constant diversion from what I must consider the central concern of criticism: the analysis and evaluation of a work of art in its integrity.

If we cross the Rhine in imagination we find, in Germany, a very different situation. One hears of existential criticism too, and, no doubt, the vocabulary of Heidegger is omnipresent, but actually German criticism today engages rather in a variety of "close reading" in obvious reaction to the speculative excesses of *Geistesgeschichte,* in a general revulsion against literary history and the grandiose constructions of the historians of the German spirit who often succumbed to the not-so-spiritual ideology of Nazism. Emil Staiger, a Swiss, is the leading practitioner of "interpretation," sensitive, learned, but as a recent speech indulging in a wholesale attack on modern literature shows, narrowly limited in taste, confined to the German classicist and romantic tradition. Staiger also tried his hand at theory. His *Grundbegriffe der Poetik* (1946) is a surprisingly schematic application of some of the oldest ideas about the distinctions between the genres: the lyrical mode is supposed to relate to the past, the epical to the present, the dramatic to the future. But Staiger is only one among the many sensitive readers of German poetry: his three-volume book on Goethe and his new book, *Stilwandel,* shows his return to the problems of literary history. He and his many academic followers can hardly be called critics in a Western sense. Criticism is either carried on in the newspapers or by a few militant Marxists who might be better called left Hegelians. They appeal to the work of Walter Benjamin who perished in 1940, an obscure, allusive writer who formulated a Marxist view of literature but was, unlike the Eastern Marxists, responsive to avant-garde tastes and modern feelings. Theodor Adorno, the editor of Benjamin and a music critic and sociologist in Frankfurt, is the acknowledged High Priest of the new left Hegelian criticism. He draws a sharp dividing line toward eastern Marxism chiding Lukács for his old-fashioned realist and bourgeois taste. He emphasizes the difference between art and reality: the work of art criticizes reality by the very contradiction between the image (which is the object received by the subject) and the reality outside (*Noten*, II, 164). Valéry, Proust, Kafka, and Beckett are his concern. Recently the new Marxism has been strengthened by emigrants from East Germany. Among them Hans Mayer is the most versatile and productive. Mayer has managed to follow the sinuosities of the party line in the East: changing, for instance, his interpretation of George Böhner from a forerunner of expressionism to a forerunner of socialist realism quite easily. But after his flight to the West he has adhered to a basic unorthodox Marxism in lovely comments on Thomas Mann, Hesse, Gerhart Hauptmann, and almost every figure of recent German literature.

Compared to the left-wing group, the right is weak if right means critics committed to a religious and conservative outlook. Hans Egon Holthusen is a genuine critic who argues from a Protestant bias for a literature which creates a reality fraught with the need for decisions and thus eminently ethical. Holthusen has criticized Rilke and Thomas Mann severely for their wrong ideas and has welcomed the position of the later Eliot.

When we go south and cross the Alps into Italy we are

again confronted with a very different cultural landscape. In Italy Croce and his followers dominated criticism for decades. They are still strong in the universities. Although their work exemplified taste and great learning, they discarded literary history and formal analysis with the result that Italian criticism, like English, offers a choice between impressionism and antiquarianism. But Croce's dominance has been on the wane since his death in 1952. In Italy most intellectuals seem to have gone over to one or the other variety of Marxism which appears often oddly combined with the aesthetic doctrines of Croce or with a revived Aristotelianism. Galvano dell Volpe, the author of a *Critica dell gusto*, was a critic of this kind. Fortunately, some Italians discovered that there are other choices available than an option for either Croce or Marx. The great German scholars of stylistics, Leo Spitzer and Erich Auerbach, made a profound impression on academic criticism: and there is now much fine analytic work which resumes the tradition of close reading, by scholars such as Gianfranco Contini who ranges from the earliest Italian sonneteers to the most "hermetic" modern poets. Besides, there is considerable interest in existentialism of the French variety of which Luciani Anceschi and his review *Aut-aut* in Milano are most fervent propagandists.

I know least about Spain. There is no public figure alive comparable to Ortega y Gasset or Unamuno. I doubt that there is much criticism. A new book by Emilia de Zuleta (*Historia de la crítica española contemporánca,* 1966) lists many fine scholars and essayists but hardly any critics. Among the scholars Damasco Alonso stands out as the practitioner of "stylistics" in the wake of the Germans, but he has, unlike them, a mystical streak. In his sensitive and ingenious book on Spanish poetry (*Poesía españolda,* 1950) he comes often to conclusions which seem to me mere gestures toward the ineffable and mysterious. Among his followers Carlos Bousono produced a well-argued *Teoría de la expresión poética* (1952).

I have left the Communist world for the last minutes of my talk. It is a very different world as there is an official creed of criticism which is imposed and enforced relentlessly. For a time there was some hope for a Thaw but even this hope is gone. The dogma of socialist realism rules supreme. Sinyavsky attacked it cogently for its blatant contradiction between the recommendation of faithful realism and the exaltation of an ideal socialism and he is in prison. Still, during the Thaw some liberalization was achieved. In Russia some interest in the Formalists active during and after the first world war was allowed to revive. The book by Mikhail Bakhtin, *Problems of the Poetics of Dostoevsky* (1929), was reprinted in 1963 and at least some scholars show the influence of the Formalist school even if they profess a general Marxism: e.g., Dmitri Likhachev, who is a specialist in Old Russian literature, has written well on the unity of form and content or on the tasks of comparative poetics or on chronicle time in Dostoevsky, topics which are taboo in orthodox Marxist criticism. Comparative literature, long a subject on the black list, is again admissable, though restricted within the limits of the Marxist dogma. In Czechoslovakia there was an even more far-reaching loosening: e.g., a book by Květoslav Chvatík on the pre-war Marxist critic Bedřich Václavek praised the avant-garde of the twenties and published pictures by such non-realists as Picasso and Léger. It slyly advocated the view that any and all kinds of modern styles may be practiced and even called "socialist realism," provided the writers are committed to Communism. It is symptomatic of the changed atmosphere, even recently before the advent of Dubček, that Jan Mukařovský, the most prominent theorist of the Prague Linguistic Circle, who had abjectly recanted in 1950, republished his early Formalist writings. In Poland for a time a more liberal outlook was possible. There are several scholars active (such as Henryk Mrakiewicz) who combine a commitment to Marxism with a genuine interest in literary problems. But Jan Kott, the interpreter of Shakespeare as our

René Wellek

contemporary, of Shakespeare as an ancestor of Beckett, of *King Lear* as anticipating *Endgame,* stays prudently away from Poland.

Emigration has not been possible for the most prominent of all Marxist critics, György Lukács in Hungary. He is by far the most influential Marxist critic in the West as he writes in German and on German and French topics. In the fifties he was branded a "deviationist," in 1956 he became Minister of Education in the short-lived government of Imre Nagy and was deported to Rumania, but he was allowed to return to Budapest and write and publish in retirement. His new two-volume *Aesthetik* seems, however, a monument of the past, an attempt to reconcile Marxism and German classicism and to combine it with Pavlovian "conditioned reflex" psychology, hampered by its doctrinaire framework and a basically nineteenth-century taste which lets him admire Thomas Mann but disapprove of everything more modern whether it be Kafka or Joyce, Eliot or Valéry. In Hungary Lukács, in his eighties, remained on the sidelines. Orthodox Marxists are in the saddle and there as well as in all the other Communist countries much scholarship (I don't say genuine criticism) is produced that manages, within its rigid framework, to reintroduce considerations of aesthetics and criticism at least in a subordinate position to its generally social and political concerns.

The map I have sketched is, I hope, multi-colored and, I fear, also sadly flat. An airplane flying at great height affords a wide view but also flattens out the landscape. Still, one has seen many things one would not see if one stayed on the ground. For some purposes airplane travel is the right way of locomotion. I hope it was for this hurried trip to Europe.

YALE UNIVERSITY

24

BRITISH CRITICISM: THE NECESSITY FOR HUMILITY

Donald Davie

As often happens, the title I have given to this lecture is the least-considered part of it. And when I saw some of the titles announced by the other speakers, I felt embarrassed at a note of what might be insular chauvinism in thus bluntly opening the proceedings with "*British* criticism." In fact I'm not aware of feeling chauvinistic about the present state of British criticism. Still less would I proffer it as a model for the rest of the world to follow. I do think, however, that the temper of British criticism is distinctive, with a distinction that we need to take note of. And conceivably it is best to note it now at the very start. For it has to do with humility, with what I take to be a properly humble conception of what the critic's role is and of how much (or rather, how little) the critic can usefully do. And I daresay it is seemly for a congregation of critics to begin by intoning a prayer that we be not puffed up but walk humbly with our God. The title that I chose so unreflectingly has one unforeseen virtue. It leaves it unclear whether I take British criticism to be a signal case of humility, or of the want of it. And I should like for a moment to leave my purpose thus uncertain. And yet if I proceed at once to name Dr. F. R. Leavis, perhaps most of you will feel that you are uncertain of my drift no longer. For even the most fervent admirers of Dr. Leavis, that great and greatly influential critic, must swallow hard before calling him a *humble* man; and of course among those many people whose reputations he has mauled, explicitly or by implication, his name is on the contrary a byword for dogmatic arrogance. So it would seem that if I were to make a case for humility as a cardinal virtue of British criticism, I should have to maintain that F. R. Leavis is an unrepresentative and eccentric figure in British criticism, just as, for instance, the late Yvor Winters can justly be thought eccentric to the distinctive temper of criticism in America. But in the case of Leavis this cannot be said; for he has been greatly influential, as Winters was not, and he could not have exerted so much influence if the temper of his criticism had been off-centre.

And yet if we dwell a little longer on the cases of Leavis in Britain and Winters in the United States, I think we find that what looks like arrogance may be humility, and vice-versa. This becomes very clear if we invoke, behind both these modern critics, the classic figure to whom both Leavis and Winters could appeal as the justifying precedent for their ways of proceeding. I mean, Dr. Johnson. For many readers even today, and for many more in the past, Johnson is the very type of unacceptable arrogance in the critic. And yet it was Johnson who wrote:

Criticism is a study by which men grow important and formidable at very little expense. The power of invention has been conferred by nature upon few, and the labour of learning those sciences which may, by mere labour, be obtained, is too great to be willingly endured; but every man can exert such judgment as he has upon the works of others; and he whom nature has made

> weak, and idleness keeps ignorant, may yet support his
> vanity by the name of a critic.

Now I will not pretend that this statement could be endorsed
by F. R. Leavis or by the many British critics of today who
model themselves upon Leavis. They are more arrogant than
Johnson was. In particular, alas, they could not easily
stomach what Johnson so explicitly insists upon—that the
critic is necessarily inferior *both* to the poet ("the power of
invention") *and* to the scholar ("the labour of learning those
sciences"). One very important emphasis does carry through,
however, from Johnson to Leavis; and it is this emphasis
which I take to be distinctive of British criticism even today,
and distinctively valuable about it. It is the assumption that
the critic is an amateur; that "the labour of learning those
sciences which may, by mere labour, be obtained" is as
foreign and unnecessary to the good critic as to the bad one.
In the present century, for Johnson's word "sciences" we
substitute the word "skills," or else the still more baleful
word "method." But in Britain as I think not elsewhere, and
certainly not in the United States, locutions like "the skills of
literary criticism" or "critical method" are still, for the most
part, highly suspect. British critics in most other respects at
odds with F. R. Leavis—I think of the late C. S. Lewis—would
agree with him that there neither is nor can be a methodology of criticism. And perhaps most of them would go so far
as to endorse his defiantly amateur definition of the critic as
simply "the good reader." There *are* no skills, there *is* no
method; and to pretend otherwise can only distract from the
one urgent prerequisite, the habit of attentiveness: this I take
to be the distinctive position of the British critic today.

The late T. S. Eliot was in nothing so completely the
naturalized Englishman as when he declared, "there is no
method except to be very intelligent." And if British critics
agree in anything, it is in repudiating any conception of

literary criticism as an arcane guild or mystery, with masters, pastmasters, initiates, acolytes, postulants, and apprentices—a conception very common indeed in the United States. But the puzzle remains—is the British critic, when he repudiates this view of himself, being more humble than his American counterpart, or more arrogant? On the one hand he is surely being, if not humble exactly, certainly unpretentious *vis á vis* his fellow-citizens. For any of them is at liberty to chance his arm in the critic's game, and this shows up very vividly for instance in the British critic's characteristic reluctance to recognize or use any sort of specialized technical terminology. (When British criticism is obscure, its obscurity derives from perversely using colloquial vocabulary and syntax on nice points of literary criticism for which colloquial language is unsuited: the telling and very curious example is William Empson, a very obscure critic and obscure because he is determined to write only tabletalk. On the other hand the British critic, as soon as he sets up in business, by that very token declares himself to be "very intelligent"; and this presumption is, if not arrogant exactly, certainly supercilious.

However, it may be that the humility or the arrogance of the critic is not to be determined by the attitude he takes up to his prospective reader, i.e. to his fellow citizens. Perhaps what we mean, when we ask whether a critic is humble enough, is whether he has a proper humility towards his predecessors, the critics of past centuries. And it's in this perspective that the characteristic temper of British criticism makes the best showing. For not Doctor Johnson only, but Sidney, Ben Jonson, Dryden, Addison, Hazlitt, Pater, and Arnold, can all be seen to have made the same assumptions about literary criticism as the contemporary British critic makes. All these critics of the British past are more or less anxiously and insistently, or else nonchalantly, amateur; in all cases their tone is that of more or less studied tabletalk, and their chosen form is the familiar essay. Even the greater solemnity of a Wordsworth or a Coleridge is the solemnity of their vocation *as poets,* which merely spills over into their criticism—which last, indeed, they seem to regard merely as a by-product of their prime commitment to poetry. Moreover, if the British critic seeks precedents further back, in the ancient world, he can maintain that Horace and "Longinus" certainly, perhaps even Aristotle also, appear to have been amateurs in just this sense. The point is brought home very sharply indeed that if we compare the British tradition in criticism with, for instance, the Italian tradition—which, from the neo-classicist legislators of the fifteenth and sixteenth centuries through to a contemporary Marxist like Franco Fortini—strikes the British reader as quite ludicrously pompous in tone and vocabulary. The great advantage of this is that very few British critics are likely to accede to the barbarous presumption otherwise rife in modern criticism—in Marxist circles certainly—but also among non- or anti-Marxists: the presumption that centuries of monkish ignorance have now at last been enlightened and that the modern critic, because he is armed with professional *method,* can do securely and convincingly in this brilliant dawn what a talented amateur like John Dryden could only grope toward uncertainly. I wish I could say that no British critic could be found subscribing to this naive view of the history of criticism as a more or less steady progress taking a sudden and momentous leap forward in our own enlightened age. Alas, I cannot claim this. But I think such an attitude is blessedly rare in British criticism; and I take Leavis's position to be in this perspective a genuinely humble one—he will be proud and well-pleased if he can discharge the function of critic in his own lifetime as well as Matthew Arnold did in his time, or Dr. Johnson in his.

However, it may be that all this is still beside the point. For it may be we should not ask whether a critic is humble or arrogant towards his masters, the critics of the past; but whether he is humble or arrogant towards the texts which he undertakes to elucidate and value. I pointed out in passing that Dr. Johnson was humble in this perspective also, insisting on the inferior status of the critical intelligence towards *inventive* intelligence which created the poems and stories to which the critic addresses himself. And I admitted that in this respect modern British criticism is sadly un-Johnsonian. This is too true. In modern Britain there is, and has been for many years, a pernicious habit of setting up what is called the literary mind against the scientific. And that expression—"the literary mind"— confounds the creative imagination of the poet with the wholly different discriminating and judicious intelligence of the critic, the poet's reader. We all know critics who are all too plainly poets *manqués*; sometimes when I read the more hasty and confident among my younger British colleagues, I suspect they think of the poet as a critic *manqué*—a heedless though gifted naïf who knows not what he does until the crucial middleman, the critic, explains his poem to the poet and his readers alike. At its ludicrous extreme this way of thinking barely and impatiently tolerates the poet (novelist, playwright, whatever) as a sort of muscular but benighted miner who has to be borne with only because he produces, fumblingly, the raw material which has to be fed into the mills of criticism from time to time just to keep them turning. This is the extreme position, never explicit. But the confusion of the creative with the critical mind lumped together under the rubric, "the literary mind," appears to be inescapable wherever literature falls under the gaze of the educator and the educational administrator. And if the confusion is particularly common and damaging in modern Britain, this is because in Britain the roles of critic and educator lie particularly close together—to the extent that many a British critic (Leavis again is a prime example) asks nothing better than to be allowed to teach literary discrimination—often enough at pre-university level.

Much of the blame for this must lie with that prototype of the critic-educator, the Inspector of Schools, Matthew Arnold. And sure enough we find in Arnold just that confusion which I have complained about, between the creative mind and the critical. Arnold's thesis—that the creative imagination flourishes best when the critical intelligence has been before it, stimulating a traffic of keen and enlightened ideas in its potential audience—seems to me not to square with the facts, so far as I can determine them, in any chapter of literary history that I have studied. It was nonetheless the crucial plank in the platform of the most influential and serious of British critical organs, Leavis's magazine *Scrutiny.* Undoubtedly it tends to establish the creative imagination and the critical intelligence dangerously near to parity, if indeed it does not make the poet virtually dependent on the critic—not indeed the critic as interpreter, but the critic as invaluable forerunner.

Other unfortunate aspects of British criticism today, other aspects of the unacceptable *arrogance* of that criticism, can also be traced back to Arnold, I suspect. But these matters may be taken up in discussion. In many cases the fault is not so much with Arnold himself as with the twist that later critics have given to Arnoldian positions. It is time to notice a particular consequence of that amateur status which Arnold, no less than British critics both before and after him, insists on. Because in this British tradition the critic is conceived of as simply the attentive reader, the British critic is characteristically unphilosophical. That is, he sees no need to find a place for his critical principles in an ambitiously systematic structure of thought which will account for and embrace such other areas as epistemology, theology, psychology. Here the tradition of the amateur is strengthened, I suppose, by the strongly empiricist temper of British thought in all fields for the last three centuries. To the Briton, criticism is something you *do,* not something you talk about doing. With the single exception of Coleridge (and of course it is a massive exception, the one that proves the rule) hardly any of the classic British critics since Philip Sidney has been interested in critical *theory,* but all have been concerned with critical practice. When a foreign observer asks in bewilderment how there can be so much practice without a theory to back it, the British critic responds impatiently *Solvitur ambulando* — these things work themselves out, all he needs and perhaps all he will trust are rules of thumb; and he may point out, justly enough and challengingly, that he has found himself enlightened on specific works by, for instance, doctrinaire Communist critics, although the theory behind their intelligent practice is such as he finds wholly unacceptable. This impatience with theory and distrust of it, this characteristic disinclination to pursue the speculative implications of the critical activity through aesthetics into psychology and epistemology, seems to fence off British criticism into a corner, out of which it is difficult for the British critic to emerge so as to engage in dialogue with critics from other cultures—who are likely to seem to him to be always discussing what criticism is, or might be, instead of getting on with it.

To this there are, or they may seem to be, two exceptions. For characteristically the British critic is all too ready to relate his criticism to two traditional areas of speculation, *viz.* politics and ethics. But in fact these exceptions are only apparent. For to the British critic politics and ethics are fields not of speculation but of action. There is, for instance, no lack in Britain of self-avowed Marxist critics; but once again it is Marxism of a notably untheoretical and unspeculative order, very much a homespun and homemade variety, in just the way indeed in which British socialism is a peculiarly insular and incurious sort of Marxism in political practice.

I have argued that British criticism today is strikingly, stubbornly faithful to a peculiarly British tradition, amateur and empiricist. But I have suggested also that in rather many ways current British criticism represents a narrowing even of its own tradition. One such impoverishment I have just alluded to, with the word "insularity"; for British criticism has not always been, and I hope will not long remain, so insular in its range and interests (bluntly, in the texts to which it addresses itself) as it tends to be today. I should like to give one further example of the narrowing of the British tradition in criticism. It turns upon the very word, "amateur." For over long stages of the history of this word in English, it has been concerned with response to other arts than literature, specifically to painting and sculpture and (less certainly) architecture. In the nineteenth century two great critics, Ruskin and Walter Pater, applied themselves to criticizing literature in the context of these other arts—just as, of course, Hazlitt and Dryden had done before them. Except for unrepresentative and uninfluential figures like the late Herbert Read, this interest has in recent years been dropped. The critic of painting, the critic of music, the critic of literature in Britain seldom talk one to another. And British criticism is poorer for the loss of this Ruskinian sweep of attention.

* * *

In my view, then, the British critic is not at all so humble as he ought to be. But then I must admit that from where I stand it seems that the French critic, the American critic, the Russian critic is, each in his own way, at least as far from a proper humility as the British critic is. And I should like in conclusion to comment, from this confessedly personal point of view, on the business of this conference and on the title that has been given to it: "Frontiers of Criticism." I am a little alarmed at the metaphor implicit in this title. For it may be taken to imply that when we call ourselves critics at the present day we are engaging ourselves in an imperial venture, thrusting deep into hostile or neutral territories and carving off new provinces to be added to the critical *imperium*. This seems to me the very opposite of that humility which I have taken to be proper and essential to the critical activity. There is no "manifest destiny" to literary criticism. It is not criticism but literature which extends frontiers; and criticism is only the camp-follower of literature. To modify the metaphor a little, there are new frontiers for criticism to advance to, wherever there is a new poem or play or story demanding to be appraised and understood. And yet even this figure does not satisfy me altogether. For I am rather more aware of territories far behind the lines, deep in the interior (as it were), which have never been cultivated by the critic at all, or else which were once cultivated but have long since reverted to wilderness. This is particularly true of the literature of the New World. The very *canon* of North American literature has never yet been established. To take a random example—Alexander Mackenzie's account of his *Voyage to the Pacific Ocean in 1793*. Is this, or is it not, a work of American literature? If not, why not? And what do we mean by asserting that it is not? Is it better or worse than dozens of other narratives of early exploration and travel in North America? These, I dare to suggest, are questions to which a properly humble criticism would address itself. I suspect they are questions which tend to be overlooked when we consider criticism in terms of its "frontiers."

STANFORD UNIVERSITY

FRONTIERS OF CRITICISM:
METAPHORS OF SILENCE

Ihab Hassan

Superfluous Preamble

The following is a small experiment in paracriticism. Some experiments neither fail nor succeed; they simply take place; and their occurrence helps to define the possible.

But what is paracriticism? Something that concerns us, I hope, as we concern ourselves with the bright, mental play of existence. If what I am doing now seems to you neither erudite nor critical, please note: I am doing it nonetheless and we are here together.

It is not a question of abandoning rational discourse; it is a question of enlarging the range of discourse; and there are those who believe that criticism should now discover some alternatives to its discursive pattern.

This preamble should be superfluous. Alas, that is not entirely the case. We all dislike those who tamper with the other into which we tempt reality. Thus the Dadaists of

Zurich drew on them as much fury as the world packed into the muddy trenches of 1917; they dared to question Art, Reason, History.

From Dada we may still learn some dadacticism. My preamble prays for an unwilling suspension of all furies. And so I begin.

I

The subject is frontiers, frontiers of criticism.

But men live perpetually in the shadow of their histories; what they call the present is already biography. Moreover, academies favor the party of Memory, and wait for culture to reveal the shape of its energies. Moreover, literature seldom moves in the far avant-garde of culture; the other arts, released from the conservative hold of language, push ahead. Finally, criticism, weighed by its own skepticism, lags still behind the literature of its day. Truly the frontiers of criticism stand somewhere between us and pre-history.

Need this always be so? The imagination is the teleological organ in evolution. It predicts change; it directs change; it fulfills change. Fantasy may become fact and dream may become history. The future we imagine conjugates our being.

Thus, a report on the frontiers of criticism may also prove an exercise in prophecy or whimsy, that is, hopefully, an exercise in metaphor. There is freedom in metaphor, incarnation, and miracle. Though I cannot presume to call metaphors into being, some may enter our discourse free.

I imagine our metaphors to be metaphors of silence. I conceive, that is, the future of art and criticism to engage new sounds of silence.

Quick Query:

Who elucidates the contemporary imagination? Is it the critics, or is it the new wandering troubadours, Leonard Cohen, Bob Dylan, Jacques Brel, John Lennon?

II

Criticism engages new sounds of silence. The engagement takes the form of metaphor.

Let us begin at the far limit of these metaphors, there where language begins to falter, and perhaps ends.

McLuhan heralds the end of print; the Gutenberg galaxy burns itself out. Electric technology can dispense with words, and language can be shunted on the way to universal consciousness. Norman O. Brown predicts that the rest is silence. The fall into language will be redeemed; "the infant of ineffable word" will lead us back to silence, our mother tongue. And Chardin, looking through the infinite perspectives of "cosmic involution," sees the universe come to rest in the form of pure thought; his Omega is wordless.

I cite these propositions not for our verification; they are merely for our edification. At a certain limit of contemporary vision, language moves toward silence. Criticism must learn to acknowledge this metaphor. Criticism must learn to define its aims with secret consent to its end. There is a peculiar wisdom that we attain only when we consent to old ends and new beginnings.

Statement:

Change is nature's way of praise, and praise the critic's way of making change possible.

III

I pass to another metaphor of silence. Language may not soon vanish into a cosmic consciousness, but it must soon respond to the new science. Fifteen years ago, Norbert Wiener suggested that languages are not "independent, quasi-biological entities, with their developments modified entirely by internal forces and needs." "In fact," Wiener said, "they are epiphenomena of human intercourse, subject to all the social forces due to changes in the pattern of that inter-course." In cybernetics, the organism is considered a pattern of messages, and messages can be coded and decoded in innumerable ways. Thus, the role of the word in mediating, in creating, the needs of culture may be radically modified.

Digression:

If the organism is a pattern of messages, man may become eventually pure information. Wiener joins McLuhan, recalls Chardin. Owen Barfield also argues that evolution can be understood only as a process of "etherealization." And Buck-minster Fuller speaks of the "ephemeralization" of society. We can already see the instruments of information—the tape recorder, the microfilm, the radio, the TV tube, the camera, the computer—become efficiently smaller, from pocket size to thumbnail size. These instruments tend to the vanishing point. Thus prophecy and technology meet.

End of Digression

But cybernetics is not the only science relevant to language, relevant to criticism. Biochemistry and neurophysiology promise to alter entirely our idea of man. Cloning, parthenogenesis, transplantation, prosthesis, the control of memory, intelligence, and behavior, the definition of genetic traits, of sex and life span, the creation of chimeras and androids; these, as Gordon Rattray Taylor says, are either here or soon to be in our midst. "Professor Jean Rostand has dramatized the biological novelty of this new man by de-scribing its characteristics: a strange biped that will combine the properties of self-reproduction without males like the greenfly; or fertilizing his female at long distances like the nautiloid mollusc; of changing sex like the xiphophores; of growing from cuttings like the earthworm; of replacing its missing parts like the newt; of developing outside its mother's body like the kangaroo and of hibernating like the hedgehog."

The result, I am sure, will prove more photogenic than Professor Rostand implies, and I hope more benevolent. But the point is this: humanism as we have known it, intermittently, for three thousand years, may no longer hold.

IV

Consider man in the Affluent Society, in a society of true plenty. There is no longer dearth and no longer necessity. There may even be no need for repression.

A society without Ananke, grim goddess of need and necessity, boggles the mind. The argument of Freud's *Civilization and Its Discontents* breaks down. Freud says this about the evolution of culture:

> The life of human beings in common therefore had a twofold foundation, *i.e.,* the compulsion to work, created by external necessity, and the power of love, causing the male to wish to keep his sexual object, the female, near him, and the female to keep near her that part of herself which has become detached from her, her child. Eros and Ananke were parents of human culture. . . .

What happens, then, when Eros and Ananke part company, when Eros remains and Ananke departs; What happens when the four-day week, to be negotiated by the unions in this decade, gives way to the one-day year, as androids or automatons do our work for us? Will these new servants, as Axel thought, also do our living for us?

How will humanism hold and how will it suffice?

Literature, perhaps more than any other art, has sustained the image of man; literature has been the carrier of humanism. And criticism, even more than literature itself, has been jealous of the letter more than the spirit of humanism.

How will criticism speak when humanism ceases to breathe? How will criticism survive? Another metaphor of silence.

V

A Recitation:

A.

Many the wonders but nothing walks stranger than man.
This thing crosses the sea in the winter's storm,
making his path through the roaring waves.

Gay nations of birds he snares and leads,
wild beast tribes and the salty brood of the sea,
with the twisted mesh of his nets, this clever man.
He controls with craft the beasts of the open air,
walker on hills. The horse with his shaggy mane
he holds and harnesses, yoked about the neck,
and the strong bull of the mountain.

Language, and thought like the wind
and the feelings that make the town,
he has taught himself, and the shelter against the cold,
refuge from the rain. He can always help himself.

B.

What a piece of work is a man! how noble in reason!
how infinite in faculty! in form and moving how express
and admirable! in action how like an angel! in appre-
    hension
how like a god! the beauty of the world! the paragon of
    animals!
And yet, to me, what is this quintessence of dust?

VI

The end of humanism need not entail the end of man.

Yet we have already felt intimations of man's sudden end as man in the landscapes of total terror. There is a silence on the other side of outrage that literature already knows. The record is in Frederick Hoffman's *The Mortal No*; the record is in George Steiner's *Language and Silence*. "Has our civilization, by virtue of the inhumanity it has carried out and condoned . . . forfeited its claim to that indispensable luxury which we call literature?" Steiner asks.

How will literature live on the lips of the inhuman? What will criticism say? Perhaps criticism can only cry: never, never, never. . . .

VII

But literature knows silences other than the inhuman imposes. The avant-garde finds ingenious ways to deny language, deny form, deny art. These ways, which often generate new kinds of art, are metaphors of silence. I have said what I know on this subject in *The Literature of Silence*. Let me briefly summarize five metaphors of anti-art:

A. Art deprecates itself. "The idea of beauty has infected us all with sickness," the Dadaists said. Art pretends now to be superfluous. Or it pretends to be absurd. "Creating or not creating changes nothing," Camus said. "The absurd creator does not price his work. He could repudiate it." High Art becomes Bunk Art. This is not "merely a passing fashion." Let us also recall that Kafka discounted his work as "scribblings," and called art a "dazzled blindness before the truth."

B. Art cancels itself. The Tinguely machine destroys itself. The blank page and the white canvas pretend to deny their existence. Sculpture is made of dry ice which melts into a puddle of water within a day. The last sentence of Beckett's *How It Is* tells us that the book is about "how it wasn't." This radical irony is implicit in the statement

· of the Cretan who pretends that all Cretans are liars. Art is no more permanent than man who may be busy canceling his traces from the universe.

C. Art becomes a game. In the foolish courts of civilization, the Fool is King. The spirit of play dominates camp, pornography, happenings. The spirit of numbers dominates the cool world of binary aesthetics. The game becomes a game of modular combinations, algebraic permutations. The forms call attention to their miraculous emptiness. Art in a "closed field," as Hugh Kenner says, draws its "dominant intellectual analogy" from "general number theory."

D. Art orders itself at random. Organic form becomes discontinuous form. The author does not impose *his* pattern on the material. He invites participation; he increases the options of men. Thus the barrier between the author and reader, creator and consumer, melts away. Both shared in discovering the world. The "Cut Up Method" of William Burroughs takes the scissors to text. The magnetic cutouts of the Swedish painter, Oyvind Fahlstrom, take the toys of the children as a model. Our galleries are filled with objects that wait upon the spectator—upon his mood, voice, shadow, or heat—to activate feedback systems and thus come to life.

E. Art refuses interpretation. Fancy pretends to be fact. Not an image of the soup can, but the soup can itself, the found object autographed. The non-fiction novel, the meditation on history, history as novel: *In Cold Blood, The Confessions of Nat Turner, Armies of the Night.* The feigned concreteness of art mutes the shrieking self. It also confesses itself helpless before the outrages of the day. No Gothic fiction is stranger than our newscasts.

But the definitive statement on anti-art is made by John Cage:

> nothing is accomplished by writing a piece of music
> nothing is accomplished by hearing a piece of music
> nothing is accomplished by playing a piece of music
> our ears are now in excellent condition

As a statement, this reveals a sacramental disposition that Cage shares with few artists. The excellence of our senses, the redemption of our consciousness, the perfection of the human community, tend to make art superfluous.

As a metaphor, however, the same quotation refers to a mixed motive lurking in neo-Dadaism, pop art, process art, funk art, computer art, concept art, *chosisme, tel quelisme,* etc.

Criticism goes slowly where literature goes. And literature, for the moment, pretends to swallow itself by the tail.

Exhortation:

Please read, on a sunny or rainy day, sitting in a rattan chair or eating a pomegranate, one, two, three, or none of the following works:

1. Philippe Sollers' *Nombres*
2. Arlene Zekowski and Stanley Berne's *Cardinals and Saints*
3. Any copy of *Aspen,* especially No. 5 + 6, in which Susan Sontag's "The Aesthetics of Silence" appears.

VIII

Aspen raises an old issue anew. The issue is mixed media, intermedia, back to Wagner and to the French Symbolists, forward to the performances of Black Mountain College, in 1952, and of Ann Halperin in 1969.

The issue is old; this does not mean that criticism has resolved it. Imagine the Magic Theatre at the Nelson Atkins Gallery in Kansas City—shades of Kafka's Natural Theatre of Oklahoma? Here is the ad for the Magic Theatre:

> How about a trip that will dissolve the floors of memory and identity, becloud the boundaries separating reality and illusion, return the traveler momentarily to his primal, psychic self—all without benefit of hallucinogens?

Imagine, say, a poetry reading in that context. Farfetched? No. At the new Electric Circus in New York, Salvatore Maritarano produced "L's G.A.," a poetry reading based on Lincoln's Gettysburg Address, projected through an amplified gas mask, to the accompaniment of tape, strobe, and film. What do we, literary critics, know that can guide our response, direct our bemusement, fashion our judgment of the case? The case is not unique. I have on my desk a novel—let us call it that—by a gifted young man—let us say gifted. It is a collection of dramatic sketches, jocular poems, aphorisms, drawings, and cutouts. It has been on my desk for some time, but my critical theory remains silent.

When I answer that young man, my voice will be personal.

IX

Two Anecdotes:

John Cage recounts two anecdotes in *A Year from Monday:*

A.

A mother and son visited the Seattle Art Museum. Several rooms were devoted to the work of Morris Graves. When they came to one in which all of the paintings were black, the mother, placing a hand across her son's eyes, said, "Come dear, mother doesn't want you to see these things."

B.

More than fifty years ago, Marcel Duchamp "called attention to the value of things to which value was not ordinarily attached." On one occasion, a CBC interviewer asked him what he was doing now. Duchamp replied: "I breathe."

X

We are moving ever closer to the traditional concerns of the critic; we are moving—stepping stones in a garden?— toward more familiar metaphors of silence.

The critic now rebels against narrow definitions of the literary response; he rebels against distinctions. His ideal is to exclude nothing from his attention.

Example:

Jerzy Kosinski is an author. He has written two extraordinary novels, *The Painted Bird* and *Steps.* Certain responses to these works, particularly to the first, remind us that the life of literature can sweep before it our discernments.

Two burly Poles appeared one day at Kosinski's doorstep. They had read *The Painted Bird,* considered it a slur on the Polish nation, and bad for the import of Polish ham. They wanted to punish Kosinski severely, and destroy the printing press that his apartment, so they thought, contained. The author practiced on them some deceptions, very similar to the deceptions his art work contained.

On another occasion, a young man sat down on the same doorstep, drinking beer and singing into the night. He could not be removed. He too had read *The Painted Bird,* considered it a work of very personal significance. The youth proved to be the editor of a college paper. He went to

Ihab Hassan

Vietnam, and wrote several times a month to Kosinski. These letters, I understand, are minor masterpieces on the arts of death.

Here is the point: fact and fiction have now become the same; and reader meets author, man to man, on the stair, on the street, on the telescreen. Moreover: the distinction between art and life is one that few contemporary artists find interesting to maintain. The academic definition of literature is, like most definitions, only part of a much larger whole.

Footnote:

Norman Holland takes a long step in the right direction when he insists, in *The Dynamics of Literary Response,* that literature is an "introjected transformation" of our fantasies. Richard Palmer and Sarah Lawall take another step when they document, in *Hermeneutics* and *Critics of Consciousness* respectively, the relevance of a phenomenological understanding of literature.
End of Footnote

The discourse of the critic, in class or quarterly, is partial; his words touch the fringes of literature. This is why the critic must seek continually to wed language and reality in some region of his awareness. This is also why the critic must learn that nothing finally needs to be said about literature.

Beyond criticism, and teleologically present in criticism, lies the silent erotics of participation, of union.

XI

A Paradox:

Abolish definitions. Offer, therefore, a definition: Literature is not a field of knowledge; it is a way, every which way, of participation.

XII

Let us continue: the next metaphor concerns discontinuity.

If we need a literary theory at all, it is a theory of discontinuity. The most vigorous thought of our day has given itself to experience the creative possibilities within continuous forms, between these forms, without these forms. This is perhaps the main point that Frank Kermode misses in his fine study, *The Sense of an Ending.* Tic toc, Kermode says, is the paradigm of time and story. But now we know that after tic may come tic again, or perhaps pst, or nothing at all.

The sense of discontinuity is hard for critics to achieve. They move along eternal typologies, guided by the Idea of organic form. Here, for instance, is Northrop Frye: "The primary understanding of any work of literature has to be based on an assumption of its unity. However mistaken such an assumption may eventually prove to be, nothing can be done unless we start with it as a heuristic principle."

This is an important, a vastly influential, statement. Unfortunately, contemporary arts do not gladly corroborate it. A novel by Burroughs, a poem by Queneau, a painting by Johns, a film by Warhol, a sculpture by Oldenburg, a piece of music by Stockhausen may share another principle. The principle is perhaps one of discontinuity. Even language begins to break as culture moves toward new centers of energy. We are not surprised to read of Marcuse's interest in the matter: "The word refuses the unifying, sensible rule of the sentence. It explodes the pre-established structure of meaning and, becoming an 'absolute object' itself, designates an intolerable, self-defeating universe—a discontinuum."

We are still used to put the text before us, and to exhaust ourselves in perceiving the intricacies of its parts. We become irate when Norman O. Brown says: "The basic assumption of modern hermeneutics, the organic unity of the document, is a commitment to univocation; and was elaborated by Protestantism to set up the one true meaning or scripture."

Criticism should learn about discontinuity and become itself less than the sum of its parts. It should offer the reader empty spaces, silences, in which he can meet himself in the presence of literature. This is the new paracriticism. This, as Brown saw, is also the method of symbolism: "To let the silence in is symbolism. 'In symbol there is concealment and yet revelation: here, therefore, by Silence and by Speech acting together, comes a double significance.' "

In discontinuity, criticism can recover the art of multivocation. Not the text and its letters but metaphors thereof. Not a form imposed but the newness between one form and another. In dreams—the testament of our broken lives—begin our responsibilities. Shatter the mirrors.

XIII

A Dream

The journey began heroically though the landscape was cluttered. The landscape offered many dangers, of time and bulk and color. He conquered without effort, without benefit of knowledge. Behind his eyes, all was lucid. But the landscape narrowed, and hairy forms closed upon him from every side. He drove ahead, clearing the path of his will. And still the landscape narrowed. Smooth walls of a cavern, veined and wet. Fear pulled at his breath. The funnel, smoother now than onyx, narrowed. For the first time, he turned around, seeking a memory of space, or light. Behind him the terrible clarity of a mirror walled his sight. He plunged again, driven now by a greater fright, and as he moved into a thin channel, scarcely larger than his head, the mirror closed behind, sealing all regress.

When he awoke, he believed all the mirrors had melted into a stream, and the sea felt fuller.

XIV

We can now move closer to the scene of contemporary criticism. The metaphors of silence are scattered in it, blank spaces in a mosaic of statements, of attitudes, of recognitions. The mosaic is not fixed in a single pattern. Every year, every decade, the pieces fall, and the pattern is made over again. The pattern itself can be seen in various ways.

I offer this random mosaic of criticism.

a. The Dutchman, Menno Ter Braak, says: "We do not proclaim ourselves for or against poetry here, we only take sides agains the deification of the form . . . at the expense of the creative being; we defend the notion that the personality is the first and last criterion in judging an artist."

b. The American, Murray Krieger, says: "Whatever our decision about the ontological status of the literary object, its existence, meaning, and value before we collide with it, we know that we can speak of it only out of the dust of that collision. We pick ourselves up, no longer quite the same selves, and try to speak with precision about what has struck us and the force of its impact. And we probably will give the usual one-sided version of what has transpired and what sort of antagonist we have encountered."

c. The Frenchman, Roland Barthes, says: "The very definition of the work changes: it is no longer an historical fact; it becomes an anthropological fact, since no history exhausts it. The variety of sense does not depend of a relativistic view of human customs; it designates, not an inclination of society to error, but a disposition of the work to openness. . . ."

d. Another Frenchman, Maurice Blanchot, says: "Literature is that experience through which consciousness discovers its being in its inability to lose consciousness . . . it reconstitutes for itself, beyond unconsciousness, a haggard knowledge, which knows nothing, which no one knows, and which ignorance finds always behind itself, like its shadow changed into a look."

e. The Swiss, Jean Starobinski, says: "In recompense, I will feel a glance arising from the work and directed on me: this glance is not the reflection of my interrogation. It is a foreign consciousness, radically other . . . the work interrogates me."

f. The German critic, Walter Benjamin, says: "With the increasing extension of the press . . . an increasing number of readers became writers. . . . It began with the daily press opening to its readers space for 'letters to the editor'. . . . Thus, the distinction between author and public is about to lose its basic character. The difference becomes merely functional; it may vary from case to case. At any moment, the reader is ready to turn into a writer. . . . Literary license is now founded on polytechnic rather than specialized training and thus becomes common property."

g. The Belgian, Georges Poulet, says: "A literary text is above all a living, conscious reality, a thought that thinks to itself and which, in thinking, becomes thinkable to us—a voice that speaks to itself and which, in so speaking, speaks to us from within."

h. Another American, Morse Peckham, says: "I have attempted to show that the notion that all works of art and all aesthetic experiences have something in common is in error, that art is a disjunctive category, established by convention, and that art is not a category of perceptual fields, but of role-playing."

i. And the great Canadian, Northrop Frye, whose heart is really not in this matter, nevertheless says: "Our society appears to be in a revolutionary phase in which the revolutionary side of the movement has been more successful than the Marxist movement of thirty years ago was in capturing the loyalties of creative and articulate people. The revolution of our time . . . is rather a psychologically based revolution, a movement of protest directed at the anxieties of privilege. . . . A revolutionary movement of this kind is one in which the arts can play a central and functional role. . . . Some issues which a generation ago were largely literary conventions have now become expanded and clarified as social issues."

Let us be clear:

I do *not* say that these critics are prophets of silence.

I do *not* say that they always confirm my sense of the frontiers of criticism

I do *not* say that they agree with one another, and form a cult or school

I do *not* say that they epitomize their critical theory in the statements I have quoted

And I do *not* say that they exhaust the range of critical opinions in the modern world.

I say that in this mosaic of statements a certain pattern or movement may be discerned. It is a movement away from the literalism of criticism, and from its former academic definition. It is a movement that explores the subjective life, the silence, of language and of consciousness, and implicates criticism into a wider experience, the fantasy of culture. It is a movement, beyond the formal control of the art object, toward the openness, and even the gratuitousness—gratuitous is free—of existence. Perhaps it is even a movement toward the generalization of our attention in an age that heralds universal leisure, the end of specialization, a movement, therefore, that seeks to adapt the literary response to new conditions of survival.

XV

The handwriting on the wall is always invisible. It becomes legible only when the wall begins to crumble.

True, my metaphors of silence may prove merely images in

a crumpled glass, traces that vanish as the beholder walks away. But I do not believe so, and the case must now come to rest in your sense of rigor and hope. There is a power in literature that enhances our presence as it recovers the infinitude of human consciousness. That same power, richly felt, adapts the future to our needs. That same power fits our will to evolution.

Let criticism, then, become paracriticism. Let it become a design for life. Let it envision a new man. Let it also praise, and thus foster mutability. This I know: at the frontiers, things come together. The frontiers are here. As Cage put it, "The purpose of one activity is no longer separate from the purpose of any other activity." Perhaps all activities are a metamorphosis that we can understand only, silently, in metaphors of love.

UNIVERSITY OF WISCONSIN–MILWAUKEE

PERSPECTIVES OF
CONTEMPORARY GERMAN CRITICISM

Victor Lange

A survey is, at best, an approximation: it is bound to reduce a rich topography to a flat outline and to distort characteristic landmarks. Like any other map it is quickly obsolete and requires constant modification. What I can offer is, therefore, only a view of those areas of recent German criticism that seem to me of interest within the purpose of this symposium.[1]

When we consider the role of criticism in Europe on the one hand and in America and England on the other, we must be struck by a curious difference between an altogether pragmatic pluralism in Anglo-Saxon critical opinion and the assertion, among European critics, of elaborately defended ideological positions, of sudden shifts in value judgments and of peremptory claims to truth. To American or English observers, criticism in France and to some extent in Germany will today appear to be obsessed by a hectic preoccupation with philosophical or historical speculation and, certainly, to be sustained by an unshakable faith in the redemptive efficacy of method.

Let me attempt to describe in what is a complex pattern of opinion and theory, a few conspicuous features of the German critical scene, and some of the methodological positions that have emerged in the wake of a widely shared reassessment of the traditional assumptions of academic as well as practical criticism.

I differentiate between practical and academic criticism because that distinction has been sharply drawn in Germany ever since the early nineteenth century.[2] With the emergence of an overwhelmingly prestigious university system in the eighteen-twenties and thirties, academic modes of critical judgment—based upon a preeminently historical theory of values and a concomitant respect for the cardinal role of philosophy—endowed the historical and aesthetic disciplines with an overriding influence on the critical practice of the century. Poetics as an aspect of aesthetics, and literary history as a mode of general historiography have in Germany provided, until our time, the compelling criteria for the study and theory of literature. The terms "literarische Kritik" or "Literaturkritik" have for long been applied to that ephemeral practice of subjective journalism that is privileged to operate without reflecting closely upon any historical or aesthetic theory. Even today "Literaturkritik" and "Literaturwissenschaft" are, in German usage, terms of very different respectability. The lengthy definition of the entry "Literaturkritik" in the apostolic *Reallexikon der deutschen Literaturgeschichte* (1960) begins with the confident sentence: "Literary criticism records our immediate reactions to literary stimuli . . . and is therefore less a form of scholarship than of journalism."[3]

It is no exaggeration to say that, with insignificant exceptions, German criticism after the 1830s was essentially determined in its topics, its principles, and its view of the function of literature by a teleological concept of history and the aesthetic assumptions, inspirational or mimetic, of a belated and increasingly frustrated classical idealism. No systematic discussion of the lyric, the "technique of the drama" (as Gustav Freytag's influential study was called) or of the novel could emancipate itself from the categorical perspectives that had been unshakably established in the three or four magisterial histories of German national literature and in the aesthetic theories expounded by Vischer (1846), Fechner (1876), and Volkelt (1897).

It was the gradual disintegration of these tenets of criticism, and the emergence, still within the academic domain, of psychological and broadly social studies (Lipps, Lamprecht, Max Weber) that provided the basis for empirical and non-speculative practices. Moreover, the attacks upon the traditional academic views of literature came, after the eighteen-seventies, with increasing effectiveness from creative writers who had found encouragement and a persuasive terminology in the theoretical reflections of the French poets from Baudelaire and Flaubert to Mallarmé and Zola. Their insistence, reinforced by the emerging social sciences, upon the role of contemporary experience in the shaping and judging of literature produced a remarkable change in the climate of German criticism: a series of militantly anti-academic journals such as *Die Gegenwart* (1872), *Die Gesellschaft* (1885), *Blaetter fuer die Kunst* (1892), or *Die Fackel* (1899) indicates the resolute dissociation of practical from traditionally academic criticism.

The academic critics remained for some time to come firmly attached to the several forms of neo-Kantian or neo-Hegelian aesthetics and to that synthetic mixture of intellectual history, psychological speculation, and vitalist philosophy that is most impressively elaborated in the work of Wilhelm Dilthey.[4] With the variety of these attitudes, and with the counter-currents of phenomenological and existentialist literary scholarship that developed between 1910 and 1930 I cannot here deal in detail. What matters for our understanding of the more recent situation of German criticism is the radical break, after 1945, with this tradition of aesthetic and historical idealism. How did that break come about and what have been the consequences for the German critical climate of the past twenty-five years?

By the turn of the century, academic criticism of the philosophical sort had in Germany lost much of its exclusive authority. A number of independent and respected critics had emerged outside the universitites, largely in the wake of Nietzsche's challenge to the accepted character and function of art and the artist. Hans Mayer (whose important role in contemporary German criticism Mr. Demetz will discuss later in this symposium) has suggested that three practicing critics determined the widely-shared attitudes toward literature. The first of these was the Austrian Karl Kraus, whose unceasing attacks on contemporary forms of intellectual and social sham sprang from basically humanist impulses. This is to say that, despite the radicalism and sharpness of his satire, the convictions that informed his cultural criticism (as well as his largely derivative poetry) were conservative and retrospective. His fervent invocation of the idealistic heritage of the German bourgeoisie was far more fascinating than the force of his analytical reasoning.[5]

The second distinct critical model was supplied by Alfred Kerr, an influential drama critic, brilliant, mannered, and impressionistic, who was so thoroughly committed to the practice of criticism that he hoped to give it the stature of a fourth literary genre. Kerr was an eminently subjective journalist, concerned with displaying the mobility and idiosyncracy of astonishing verbal gifts in the defense, not, like Kraus, of threatened historical values but, on the contrary, of a totally contemporary sensibility.[6]

The third among these exemplary critics (and perhaps the least known) was Herbert Jhering, in the twenties and thirties Kerr's chief antagonist and an eloquent advocate of the political theater of Barlach and Brecht, of Heinrich Mann, and, significantly, of the new medium of the film.[7]

It is an obvious, though useful, simplification to suggest that these critics represented three different intellectual complexions—traditional, contemporary, and "revolutionary"; that they attacked for nearly a quarter of a century the time-honored notion of literature—and criticism—as an elevated and privileged enterprise, and that each was in his own way intensely preoccupied with the rhetorical devices that determine the social effectiveness of literature.

Although that same political and cultural totalitarianism against which Krauss, Kerr, and Jhering had directed their retrospective, impressionist, and analytical criticism succeeded during the Nazi period, it is nevertheless apparent that something like their points of view, though now in a different political context, was reiterated after the second world war. Hans Egon Holthusen was the first of the younger post-war critics who articulated in his essays and, indirectly through his anthology of contemporary poetry, *Ergriffenes Dasein* (1953), a conservative, cautiously neo-classicist, sometimes metaphysically oriented criticism.[8] He found his sustaining model in T. S. Eliot, and his target in Thomas Mann's ironic philosophy; he was the most appealing advocate of a prescriptive view of literature, and of poetry as a means of access to religious or spiritual meaning. This critical faith was widely challenged as "traditionalist" or even (in the curious language of the day) as "affirmative" and soon lost much of its early appeal.

A second group of German post-war critics may—in full awareness of their different historical position and their far less spectacular manner—be discretely put in parallel to the "impressionist" sensibility of Alfred Kerr. Among these I would include K. Krolow, I. Bachmann, R. Baumgart, and Helmut Heissenbuettel, poet-critics who contributed to the several Frankfurt seminars on literary theory and who have been preeminently concerned with issues of poetic procedure.[9] It would be quite misleading to speak of their criticism as formalist; yet, they are on the one hand suspicious of the "spiritualist" aesthetics of the Kraus-Holthusen persuasion, and on the other careful to detach themselves from the third and most aggressive group of critics, writers like H. M. Enzensberger, Martin Walser, or M. Reich-Ranicki, who insist upon practicing criticism in the context of contemporary political realities and therefore in close relationship to the findings of the social sciences. In their essays we find distinct (but not specifically Marxist) parallels to the attitudes of Jhering.[10] This form of criticism is neither retrospective nor, strictly speaking, devoted to an understanding of the aesthetic properties of a text; it is rather directed at the opportunities which literature offers for a transformation of the society in which it exists.

Some of these convictions are similar, of course, to interests and positions that were previously or concurrently formulated by influential poets, novelists, or playwrights such as Benn and Loerke and their views of the lyrical procedure; or Doeblin, Mann, and Musil on the resources and forms of fiction; or Brecht, Duerrenmatt, and Max Frisch on the role of the new theater. All of these, however different their premises, were agreed that the work of art represents modes of access to cognition, that they should disavow all Platonic metaphysics and, certainly—except for Brecht—any aesthetics of mimesis. They reflected, above all—and this is a dominant issue of much recent German criticism—an overriding interest in problems of language. The consequences and applications which this concern has produced are too complex to describe in a brief survey; they elaborate in one way or another that experience of a disturbed relationship between language and reality which Hofmannsthal's "Ein Brief" first explored and described in 1902. The range of these critics extends from a delineation of the special function of the poetic language in

Gottfried Benn's theory of the lyric to an examination of the ideological deceptions of language (Enzensberger, Emrich) and the German contributions (seldom without reference to Wittgenstein or Jakobson) to the current debate on linguistics, stylistics, poetics, and rhetoric.[11] Here, too, incidentally, the metaphysical or affirmative, the formal or poetological, and the analytical tendencies of which I spoke earlier, appear to be the prevalent modes. (The most interesting demonstration of this unremitting testing of the functions of language is to be found in the prose texts of Juergen Becker and Peter Handke as well as in a discursive debate on the relationship of language and reality between H. Heissenbuettal and H. Vormweg.)[12]

These poets and critics agree upon a number of other presuppositions as well: They appear unwilling to inquire into the nature of the poetic experience, that is, the character of the imagination, or into the effect of a text upon the individual—as against the collective—sensibility. In striking contrast to the important English or American critics, they are therefore almost totally uninterested in psychological or psychoanalytical approaches, either in Freudian terms or in Jungian mythological patterns of the archetypal imagination. What has engaged nearly all post-war German critics—clearly as a reaction to the mass of speculative, spiritualistic, and mythographic criticism before 1945—is the problem of the public effectiveness of literary works, either within a given social and philosophical context or in deliberate isolation from it.

I have so far spoken of the remarkably energetic and diverse activities of the practical critics. It may be said that without these, and without their hostility to traditional historical approaches, the divorce of German academic criticism itself from its intellectual assumptions, and the turning from aesthetic speculation toward literary theory would hardly have occurred. The varieties of *Geistesgeschichte* and other neo-idealistic methods that developed between the wars had, it is true, proved to be increasingly removed from the contemporary philosophical and scientific climate. [13] Dilthey, from his position of historical vitalism, equated poetic production with an intense projection of a "sense of life" and elaborated large and elusive typologies of styles, attitudes, movements, and ingenious syntheses. He and his successors (Petersen, Walzel, or Gundolf) were inclined to be skeptical of empirical procedures and of attaching decisive importance to poetological categories. "Criticism does not begin," said Fritz Strich in one of his later studies, "until we become indifferent to the text as such." [14] In the hands of such critics, the work of art tended to evaporate or to be consumed in the pursuit of a perennial human essence that maintained itself with only incidental historical adjustments throughout the ages. The distaste for pseudo-historical constructions and a suspicion that they had helped to produce the ideological ethos that culminated under the Nazis in an "affirmative" view of criticism coincided after the war with an aversion to any kind of unifying theory of history validating the critical act.

Two or three unconvincing efforts made it clear that the writing of literary history of a comprehensive sort encountered doubts and difficulties that could not be taken lightly. Once the construct of a synthesizing system (such as Josef Nadler, the last grand prestidigitator, achieved in his *Literaturgeschichte des Deutschen Volkes,* 4th ed. 1939) was recognized as a fascinating but artificial dramatic spectacle, it was only the history of particular forms or the compilation of annalistic or encyclopedic surveys that remained feasible. Literary history had plainly ceased to provide an adequate system of description or evaluation.

It is not surprising that in reaction to these critical and historical (as well as implicitly political) scruples, German academic critics should have joined the practical in a demand for more specific attention to the text itself and to the forms of access to it. Two handbooks of criticism determined much of the post-war literary scholarship in Germany. One was Emil Staiger's *Grundbegriffe der Poetik* (1946), which re-asserted certain tenets of classical aesthetics, especially a theory of genres, that were indebted to Goethe's notion of "natural" typological forms. Combined with Heidegger's ontological view of the three states of temporality, they produced Staiger's definition of "lyrical," "epic," and "dramatic" attitudes and led to his projection of corresponding stylistic principles. An admirable critical perception enabled Staiger to offer subtle interpretations of individual works (*Die Kunst der Interpretation,* 1955) but the fundamentally traditionalist character of his position emerged ever more rigid, and not long ago involved him in an angry polemic against all forms of "modernist" writing and criticism.

The other and more fundamental attempt at a comprehensive theory of literature was Wolfgang Kayser's *Das Sprachliche Kunstwerk* (1948), a work, like Staiger's, written outside Germany during the war and with a remarkably close awareness of the formal and formalist theories that had developed in Russia and later in the United States. Kayser sharply focused upon the linguistic and structural characteristics of the literary text; he adopted some of the critical principles that German historians of art such as A. Riegl and M. Dessoir had formulated earlier, and insisted on the specifically aesthetic nature of the literary work.[15]

Kayser's "intrinsic criticism" and its all-pervasive influence during the past twenty years has recently come under attack from those who have accused him of "formalism"; but there can be no doubt of its effects. It produced a series of studies, by Kayser himself and others, in which the classical genres—ballad, satire, elegy, comedy, etc.—were subjected to specific rhetorical and poetological scrutiny; it created a fresh interest in the formal features of modern European poetry; it suggested the perspectives of E. Laemmert's *Bauformen des Erzaehlens* (1955) which explicitly rejects any generic notion of "the novel" in favor of a descriptive analysis of various narrative devices; it turned the attention of younger critics to the formal features of allegory, metaphor, and symbol; and it was instrumental in drawing a number of scholars toward recognizing the interdependence of linguistics and poetics. Broadly speaking, Kayser stimulated and confirmed a tendency—especially appealing as an antidote to the German propensities for spiritual generalization—toward empirical criticism, an interest at once strengthened and sensibly tempered by René Wellek and Austin Warren's *Theory of Literature*, which appeared in a German translation in 1959.

The counter-arguments to this "intrinsic" or "immanent" approach that have been advanced by recent German critics have reiterated the pattern of scrutiny, modification, or opposition that has emerged to similar formal theories in England, France, or America. The debate has concerned itself with several large issues: the first focuses upon the need of a historical framework within which the literary text in its recognized aesthetic mode should be illuminated more adequately than formal criticism considers feasible. This demand is as plausible as it is fraught with methodological difficulties: a survey such as Paul Boeckmann's *Formgeschichte der deutschen Dichtung* (1949) showed the difficulties inherent in a comprehensive enterprise in which a description of the historical function of the literary text, however carefully defined in its formal characteristics, remains nevertheless dependent upon successive phases of general and historical awareness. Historical and formal criticism have been more legitimately joined in some German studies in which a given period-context has been clarified and specified by an empirical attention to the formal modifications of genres or of rhetorical conventions. R. Brinkmann's of P. Demetz's attempts at determining the distinct literary features of realism, or G. R. Hoche's and M. Thalmann's examination of manner-ism, have offered persuasive models of such an inquiry.[16]

The second and more radical challenge to "intrinsic" criti-cism has come from those who have found that methodologi-cal procedure altogether inadequate for a definition of the function of literature and, indeed, of criticism itself. Intrinsic criticism seems only indirectly to pay attention to the socio-logical premises of literature and of literary judgment. The central intention of criticism should be, argue the anti-intrinsic critics, to perform a critique precisely of those ideological implications or limitations of a text that are likely to remain unreflected in a strictly aesthetic procedure. Hans Mayer's numerous studies have shown how social and formal impulses should in an effective act of criticism be related. [17] Th. Adorno and W. Emrich, both ontological critics with different philosophical convictions (the one empirical, the other more idealistic, but both in the succession of W. Ben-jamin), have asserted these scruples most energetically.[18]

This form of "anti-ideological" criticism has recently exercised an extraordinary appeal; it has produced an un-mistakable idiom and a passionate, often single-minded enthusiasm, especially for the dialectical mode of Th. Adorno. As a Hegelian and Marxist, anti-phenomenologist and anti-existentialist, Adorno has in occasional essays on the contemporary condition of fiction or poetry, on Balzac, Proust, or Valéry, argued his thesis that the great documents of modern literature reveal the paralyzing character of a disfigured and dehumanized world which can only be made transparent, intelligible, and tolerable in a "poetic" rendering of its inherent contradictions.

But Adorno's or Emrich's critical stance is only one of several attempts at moving beyond the intrinsic procedure toward an analytical view of the historical character of litera-ture and an explicit concern with literary value judgments. To this third issue of contemporary German criticism several studies have addressed themselves with varying degrees of detachment. W. Muller-Seidel and F. Sengle have tended to look back, with humane feelings for the fundamental importance of history, upon the lost certainties of an affirmative historical or philological idealism. H. E. Hass and Max Wehrli have attempted judicious analyses of the issues. [19] W. Kayser himself maintained, in *Wahrheit der Dichter* (1959), a certain formalist skepticism. But all of these have recognized that no sufficient theory of literary judgment can be established without a clear view of the unique character of the literary text and of the specific means of understanding it. Criticism, they have insisted, must above all be intent upon the nature of the critical process itself. And to develop a theory of criticism from its hermeneutical preconditions is the fourth and perhaps the most important concern of much contemporary German criticism. It is the most important because it takes cognizance of the critical alternatives and difficulties outlined above, and because it inevitably involves decisions as to the historical as well as the aesthetic character of the literary text.

Two or three works have played a conspicuous role in this hermeneutical debate: the late Roman Ingarden's ontological examination of the work of art, *Das Literarische Kunstwerk* (2nd ed. 1960), against whose phenomenological dissociation of structure and value (in the 1st ed. 1931) R. Wellek has sharply argued in his *Theory of Literature,* was recently followed by a systematic study of the modes of aesthetic judgment. [20] Ingarden is as radically anti-psychological as he is, of course, anti-historical, and his position is exceedingly abstract in its discrimination between artistic and aesthetic values. It is, indeed, far more so than a work of equal or even greater influence upon contemporary German criticism, Käthe Hamburger's *Die Logik der Dichtung* (1957). Miss Hamburger detaches the determinants of the literary text from the general literary aesthetics and maintains that the logical functioning of language in producing literary statements determines the functioning of literary forms. The critical issue which her study has raised is, of course, related to the fundamental question of the kind of knowledge that is required for an appropriate understanding of the literary text. [21] And to this question both H. G. Gadamer's *Wahrheit und Methode* (1965) and Peter Szondi's essay "Uber philologische Erkenntnis" address themselves within a wide philosophical and historical context. [22] Gadamer develops a theory of understanding in which the interpretation of literary texts is made dependent upon a comprehension of the historical accretions of its language and of the tradition of critical judgment that the work has produced. Indebted to Dilthey as well as to Heidegger, Gadamer's book offers in Germany at the moment the most serious analysis of the hermeneutical issue.

Szondi in turn denies the possibility of any phenomenological access to the literary text; he rejects "intentional" aesthetics and insists, in the spirit of Valéry, Stefan George, or Walter Benjamin, upon the unique, multivalent character of the work, which must not be delimited by scientific or historical generalizations. Its potential meaning, independent of any poetic intention, can only emerge in the pursuit of philological criticism and in a scrupulous examination of previous acts of interpretation.

If Szondi's inquiry into the specific epistemological character of the act of literary criticism and its hermeneutical premises reflects a central topic of contemporary German criticism, it is largely because the two dominant critical systems of the recent past, Marxist and formalist criticism, have shown themselves incapable of providing historical terms sufficiently comprehensive for an adequate theory of understanding. To a discussion of this comprehensive understanding of the historical scope of criticism, a considerable amount of attention has recently been devoted. Perhaps the most elaborate summary of this issue has been given in what seems to me a compelling essay by H. R. Jauss, dramatically entitled *Literaturgeschichte als Provokation der Literatur-wissenschaft* (1967).[23] Let me, in conclusion, outline the argument of this stimulating paper.

What Marxist and formalist criticism have in common, Jauss asserts, is a rejection of positivism as well as of the metaphysical implications of *Geistesgeschichte*. Each deals with the problem of the sequentiality of literary works in its own unsatisfactory way. A Marxist interpretation of literature derives its historical categories from an overriding faith in social evolution and (at best) extracts from the literary constellations of the past preliminary—or exemplary—modes of social insight. Marxist literary historiography and criticism operate within categories of national and economic experiences and these represent only a small measure of the total aesthetic complex. There are other difficulties: Werner Krauss, the most distinguished literary historian in East Germany, has pointed to the impossibility of doing justice, within a Marxist theory of literary history, to the heterogeneity of contemporary works;[24] and P. Demetz as well as R. Wellek have shown that the stubborn classical assertion of an identity of form and content (e.g., in the mirror-theory of (Lukács) has made it impossible for Marxist criticism to develop a theory of literature sufficiently sophisticated to protect nearly all modern art from being dismissed as bourgeois and decadent.[25]

The theory of formalism, on the other hand, at least in its earlier phases, deliberately aimed at removing the literary object from its historical determinants and defined its efficacy functionally, as the sum total of all its artistic devices. The distinction made by formalist criticism between poetic and nonpoetic features of a text requires of the critical act an awareness of the specific formal characteristics of a given work and its relative character in a series of comparable products. It is true that in admitting a synchronic relationship between poetic and non-poetic modes of literature, and in admitting a diachronic relationship of works and genres (and thus an evolutionary succession of aesthetic systems, of forms and genres), later formalist critics have moved closer to providing a possible scheme of historical judgment. But to understand a literary text within the limits of the history of its particular formal systems is not the same as understanding it within the more comprehensive categories of, for instance, its production, its social function, or its historical consequences. A general history of literature can therefore hardly be conceived as a succession of formal systems. Like language itself, the literary text must be comprehended as a specific structure as well as a historical phenomenon, but, beyond the diachronic or synchronic succession of its forms, within the larger context of a general history.

Jauss and several of his colleagues at the University of Konstanz [26] have argued that both Marxism and formalism are bound to remain enclosed in self-imposed historical insufficiency and that their methods can achieve an understanding of the literary work only with an aesthetic of production and representation. In neither theory, they insist, is the factor of reception and impact, the factor of reader, listener, or spectator sufficiently taken into account. Marxist criticism regards the reader, if at all, as virtually identical with the author, and is, at best, concerned with identifying his place in a given society. Formalism, on the other hand, requires the reader only as a perceiving subject who follows the directions of the text and differentiates formal characteristics and features. In both systems of criticism the reader operates with a quasi-scientific sort of attention. But literary texts are not, as a rule, written to be read and judged by philologists or social scientists; they transmit information to a suitably perceptive recipient and are designed to produce a constant interaction of question and answer. This relationship between

67

the work and its readers is of considerable consequence for our understanding of literature; it has aesthetic as well as historical implications: even the earliest reception of a work of art by a reader demands evaluative judgments derived from a familiarity with comparable works or procedures; and the reception by a first reader is only the first in a chain of receptive acts, each more elaborate than the previous one, and therefore contributing to our understanding of the historical significance as well as the aesthetic potential of a given work.

It is in this dimension, then, of reception and effect that the historical as well as the aesthetic judgment must be brought into play, and it is this double perspective that distinguishes Jauss's procedure from any traditional *Wirkungsgeschichte.* From the general premise of an aesthetic concerned with the reception of a literary text, Jauss has argued the case for a new conception of general literary history. The categories by which such a history of literature should be developed, he maintains, must inevitably be concerned with the successive experiences of readers; and to record and evaluate the history of the critical reception of a work is the task (eminently "philological" in the sense of classical hermeneutics such as that of August Boeckh) of a theory of literature that is aware of immanent as well as historical procedures. Indeed, Jauss concludes, a literary text can be said to reveal its character—or meaning—only by the evidence of its successive historical effects.

A text cannot function objectively and independent of its readers; for, unlike a political event, a poem has no necessary consequences, it continues resonant only in so far as it is received and judged by its readers. It is one of Jauss's important—though surely questionable—convictions that the mode of reception can be objectively defined by an analysis of the manner in which a work meets the expectations of its readers—expectations emerging from available forms, genres, themes, linguistic structures, etc.—that is to say, of the response to explicit or implicit "signals" contained in the work itself. Novels such as *Don Quixote, Tristam Shandy, Werther,* or *Sentimental Education* mobilize the reader deliberately within what Jauss describes as an intended "horizon" of critical behavior. How a work is received at the point of its first appearance as well as subsequently, whether it surpasses, disappoints, or refutes, whether it challenges or merely confirms prevalent expectations, should permit conclusions even as to its quality. What is important for such an aesthetic of reception is the mutual exercise of challenge and response; the challenge of a work which, without claiming any fixed meaning, yet contains a variety of objectively describable aesthetic stimuli; and the responses of a succession of readers who bring their particular perception (and philological or rhetorical assumptions) to bear upon the accumulated critical experience of previous readers, and who thereby in turn "define" the work as well as their own historical situation.

In an elaboration of Erich Auerbach's analysis of the French public in the seventeenth century, Jauss (and similarly Harald Weinrich with his plea for a literary history of the reader)[27] attempts to go far behind Levin Schuecking's concept of the sociology of literary taste which assumes a specific public that is subject to historical and sociological description. There are undoubtedly works which, when they appear, cannot be related to any given public; they are so thoroughly outside an existing "horizon" that a public can only slowly form around them. A history of the successive responses to a text is therefore indispensable for an understanding, particularly of the more remote texts.

Some of Jauss's theses are, of course, related to a variety of modern philosophical premises: to Heidegger's notion of temporality as well as to Mannheim and Husserl (who first used the term "horizon of expectation") and to Siegfried Krakauer who, in a paper entitled "General History and the

Aesthetic Approach," has questioned the usefulness of any general history, that is, of a diachronic form of historical description. In *Wahrheit und Methode* Gadamer has suggested that the historical character of all interpretation can be adequately demonstrated only through an understanding of the history of successive aspects of the experienced text. Such a procedure must not isolate the text as an object but, on the contrary, show the unfolding of a potential of meaning that is virtually given in the work, historically actualized in its reception and made concrete in the history of its relevance.

If Jauss's concept challenges a widely held skepticism toward any analysis that assumes that the expectations of the reader can in fact be objectively determined, it rejects with equal conviction the current variations of typological or mimetic theory from which Northrop Frye or the French structuralists have derived their conclusions. Whatever counter-position may be asserted by Jauss's critics, his scheme is undoubtedly open to at least one cardinal question: can the suggested procedure be effectively applied to more than a limited number of conspicuous and amply documented major texts and is it, therefore, likely to yield a useful prescription for the unfolding of a spacious and comprehensive history of literature?

Jauss reflects, in any case, the continuing concern of German criticism with the historical ambience that determines a literary text; he deals, perhaps more satisfactorily than Emil Staiger in his study of stylistic change, with the issue of the succession of literary sensibilities. While he puts little faith in the appropriateness of an analysis of the creative process for our understanding of the work of art, he emphasizes the importance, for any theory of literary criticism, of historical categories adequate to the aesthetic character of the work of art.

PRINCETON UNIVERSITY

NOTES

1. Leonard L. Duroche, *Aspects of Criticism: Literary Study in Present-Day Germany* (New York: Humanities, 1967). Jost Hermand, *Synthetisches Interpretieren: zur Methodik der Literaturwissenschaft* (München: Nymphenburg, 1968). Eric Lunding, *Strömungen und Strebungen der modernen deutschen Literaturwissenschaft,* Acta Jutlandica, XXIV, 1 (Aarhus: Universitetsforlaget, 1952). Hans Mayer, ed., *Deutsche Literaturkritik im Zwanzigsten Jahrhundert* (Stuttgart: Goverts, 1965).

2. Peter Uwe Hohendahl, "Literaturkritik und Öffentlichkeit," *Zeitschrift fur Literaturwissenschaft und Linguistik,* I (1971), p. 40. Edgar Lohner, "Tradition und Gegenwart deutscher Literaturkritik," *Sprache im Technischen Zeitalter,* III (1962), 238-248.

3. Werner Kohlschmidt and Wolfgang Mohr, "Literarische Kritik," im Merker-Stammler *Reallexikon der Deutschen Literaturgeschichte,* eds. W. Kohlschmidt and W. Mohr, 2nd. ed., II, 63-79.

4. Herbert Hodges, *The Philosophy of Wilhelm Dilthey* (London: Routledge, 1952). Kurt Müller-Vollmer, *Towards a Phenomenological Theory of Literature: A Study of Wilhelm Dilthey's "Poetik"* (The Hague: Mouton, 1963). René Wellek, "Wilhelm Dilthey," in Vol. IV of *A History of Modern Criticism* (New Haven: Yale Univ. Press, 1965). pp. 320-335.

5. Karl Kraus, *Werke.* 10 Vols. (München: Kösel, 1954-1960).

6. Alfred Kerr, *Die Welt im Drama*, ed. Gerhard F. Hering, 2nd ed. (Köln: Kiepenheuer, 1966).

7. Herbert Jhering, *Von Reinhardt bis Brecht: Vier Jahrzehnte Theater und Film.* 3 Vols. (Berlin: Aufbau Verlag, 1958-61).

8. Hans Egon Holthusen, *Ja und Nein: Neue Kritische Versuche* (München: Piper, 1954); *Kritisches Verstehen* (München: Piper, 1961); *Der unbehauste Mensch* (München: Piper, 1951); *Das Schöne und das Wahre* (München: Piper, 1958).

9. Reinhard Baumgart, *Aussichten des Romans oder hat Literatur Zukunft?* (Nieuwied: Luchterhand, 1967). Helmut Heissenbüttel, *Über Literatur* (Olten: Walter, 1966). Karl Krolow, *Aspekte zeigtenössischer deutscher Lyrik* (Gütersloh: Mohr, 1961).

10. Hans Magnus Enzensberger, *Einzelheiten* (Frankfurt: Suhrkamp, 1962). Marcel Reich-Ranicki, *Literatur der kleinen Schritte* (Munchen:

Piper, 1967). Martin Walser, *Erfahrungen und Lesererfahrungen* (Frankfurt: Suhrkamp, 1965).

11. Max Bense, *Theorie der Texte* (Köln: Kiepenheuer E Witsch, 1962). Helmut Kreuzer and R. Gunzenhauser, eds., *Mathematik und Dichtung* (München: Nymphenburger Verlagshandlung, 1965). Herbert Seidler *Allgemeine Stilistik* (Göttingen: Vandenhoeck & Ruprecht, 1953).

12. Helmut Heissenbüttel und Heinrich Vormweg, *Briefwechsel über Literatur* (Neuwied: Luchterhand, 1969).

13. Paul Boeckmann, "Von den Aufgaben einer geistesgeschichtlichen Literaturbetrachtung," *DVjS,* (IX (1931), 448-471. Karl Viëtor, *Literaturgeschichte als Geistesgeschichte,"PMLA,* LX (1945), 899-916. Kurt May, "Zu Fragen der Interpretation," *DVjS,* XXXIII (1959), 608-644.

14. Fritz Strich, *Kunst und Leben* (Bern: Francke, 1960), p. 7.

15. Gerhard Storz, "Wendung zur Poetik," *Der Deutschunterricht,* II (1952), 69-83.

16. Richard Brinkmann, ed., *Begriffsbestimmung des literarischen Realismus* (Darmstadt: Wissenschaftliche Buchgesellschaft, 1969). Richard Brinkmann, *Wirklichkeit und Illusion: Studien über Gehalt und Grenzen des Realismus für die erzählende Dichtung des 19. Jahrhunderts,* 2nd ed. (Tübingen: Niemeyer, 1966). Peter Demetz, *Formen des Realismus: Theodor Fontane* (München: Hauser, 1964). Gustav Rene Hoche, *Manierismus in der Literatur* (Hamburg: Rowohlt, 1959). Marianne Thalmann, *Romantik und Manierismus* (Stuttgart: Kohlhammer, 1963).

17. Hans Mayer, *Zur deutschen Literatur der Zeit* (Reinbeck: Rowohlt, 1967).

18. Theodor W. Adorno, *Noten zur Literatur* 3 Vols. (Frankfurt: Suhrkamp, 1958-65). Wilhelm Emrich, "Zum Problem der literarischen Wertung," *Abhandlungen der Mainzer Akademie der Wissenschaften und Literatur, Klasse Lit., 1961.* Walter Müller-Seidel, *Probleme der Literarischen Wertung,* 2nd ed. (Stuttgart: Metzler, 1969). Jochen Schulte-Sasse, *Literarische Wertung* (Stuttgart: Metzler, 1971).

19. Hans Egon Hass "Das Problem der literarischen Wertung," *Studium Generale,* XII, 1959, 727-756. Max Wehrli, *Allgemeine Literaturwissenschaft* (Bern: Francke, 1951).

20. Roman Ingarden, *Erlebnis, Kunstwerk und Wert* (Tübingen: Niemeyer, 1969); *Das literarische Kunstwerk,* 3rd. ed. rev. (Tübingen: Niemeyer, 1966); *Vom Erkennen des literarischen Kunstwerks* (Tübingen: Niemeyer, 1968).

21. Käthe Hamburger, *Die Logik der Dichtung* (Stuttgart: Klett, 1957); *Philosophie der Dichter* (Stuttgart: Klett, 1966).

22. Hans Georg Gadamer, *Kleine Schriften* 2 Vol. (Tübingen: Mohr, 1967). Peter Szondi, "Über philosophische Erkenntnis," in *Hölderlin-Studien* (Frankfurt: Insel, 1967). pp. 9-30.

23. Hans Robert Jauss, *Literatur als Provokation* (Frankfurt: Suhrkamp, 1970).

24. Wolfgang Iser, ed., *Immanente Ästhetik-Aesthetische Reflexion* (München: Fink, 1966). Hans Robert Jauss, ed., *Nachahmung und Illusion* (München: Fink, 1969). Hans Robert Jauss, ed., *Die nicht mehr schönen Künste* (München: Fink, 1968).

25. Harald Weinrich, "Für eine Literaturgeschichte des Lesers," *Merkur,* XXI (1967), 1027-1038.

26. Siegfried Krakauer, "General History and the Aesthetic Approach," in *Die nicht mehr schonen Künste,* ed. Hans Robert Jauss, (München: Fink, 1968), pp. 111-127; 560-581.

27. Emil Staiger, *Stilwandel: Studien zur Vorgeschichte der Goethezeit* (Zürich: Atlantis, 1963).

TRANSFORMATIONS OF RECENT MARXIST CRITICISM: HANS MAYER, ERNST FISCHER, LUCIEN GOLDMANN

Peter Demetz

Three branches of modern thought (Marxism, psycho-analysis, and formalism in its various guises) have challenged criticism in the first half of our century but the Marxist critics had to pass more severe tests than others. The alliance of criticism with institutionalized state power, in the Soviet Union and elsewhere, did little to further courage and sophis-tication; and even George Lukács found himself often caught in the rituals of prescribed self-castigation. Yet the sharp contours of recent changes cannot be ignored: political rigid-ity has been replaced in many places by a volatile polycen-trism coinciding with tangible unrest in intellectual debate; official Soviet Marxism-Leninism has fallen upon lean years, and the young intellectuals in the former Moscow sphere of influence are turning to new combinatory interpretations of Marxism which are to be humanist, liberal, creative. Philos-ophers in Warsaw, Budapest, Zagreb (and among the exiled Prague reformers) are now calling for intellectual spontaneity again: Karel Kosík and Ivan Sviták among the Czechs; Adam

Schaff and Lezsek Kolakowski in Poland; Miklos Almasi in Budapest; and the intellectually high-powered circle around the Zagreb philosophical journal *Praxis,* which is continuing in its own fashion what the Leipzig *Deutsche Zeitschrift für Philosophie* began in the early 1950s under the aegis of Ernst Bloch and Walter Harich. The discussion of modern alienation and the new role of the individual in the socialist state provides a context in which a Fifth International of humane Marxism can define its new and flexible ideas with visionary energy.

But it is difficult to ignore the paradox that new Marxist literary criticism develops richly in the industrial countries of the West rather than in more strictly planned societies. The old bourgeois order, in parliamentary democracies, may have many deficiencies, but apparently not the one of inhibiting Marxist critics who are refining their thought. I can only describe this phenomenon, not explain it: perhaps the younger Marxist intellectuals would rather concern themselves at this moment with sociology than with *belles lettres;* or we attach perhaps too little importance to the consequences of their actual experience with their governments. Even hesitant relaxation of rigidity often causes the young literary critics of the Communist world to move away from Marxism rather than toward it—as in the case of Mikhail Bachtin or the Czech scholar and critic Jiří Levý who was returning to the traditions of the Prague Linguistic Circle and its formalist orientation. But I am not a Hegelian trying to project the course of the abstract *Weltgeist* and should like to confine myself to a more concrete view of the new possibilities, developed by literary critics in the age of the Marxist "Thaw." It is hard to make a representative choice, but I am inclined to believe that the essays of Hans Mayer, Ernst Fischer, and Lucien Goldmann imply three potential escapes from traditional orthodoxy. I am trying to follow the trail of these three critics, long known in Europe and, more recently, increasingly discussed in American universities, and I am even willing to risk the discovery that innovation occasionally reveals itself as return to older ideas or leads to those self-critical frontiers where Marxism abruptly begins to investigate its own assumptions again.

*   *   *

The inhuman events of recent history have sharpened rather than diminished Hans Mayer's commitment to literary criticism. As refugee, editor-in-chief of an American radio in occupied Germany, professor at the Karl-Marx University in Leipzig, spokesman for cultural liberalization in East Germany, professor in Hannover, translator, musician, television star, world traveler, and last polymath of the Weimar Republic, Mayer rarely hesitated to combine the most conflicting loyalties. His sharp intelligence is directed toward discovering the Hegelian *Weltgeist* in history but his highly civilized and receptive aesthetic sensibility enjoys the pleasing textures of literature and music. A connoisseur in the culinary tradition, Mayer has avoided more energetically than Lukács the blindness caused by *a priori* systems and welcomes the impact of those "sense data" which, according to Hermann Hettner, "demand appreciation on their own."

Disinclined to submit himself to an abstract history of ideas or to aesthetic formalism, Mayer pleads for the renewal of historical and social orientations. Literature is, after all, *inextricably involved with history, and the literary historian constantly confronts connections between his field and the realm of matter; literary history becomes a component of general history—though a highly self-sufficient and, in many respects, self-centered one.* Mayer's account of the relationship between literature and the material elements of history wavers (as did that of Marx and Engels) between an idea of linear causality and a loose concept of interaction between history and the creative intellect. Mayer proceeds from the entire spectrum of possibilities worked out in the first half of the nineteenth century by thinkers ranging from Mme de Staël to Marx. Sometimes literature *expresses* society, as Mme de Staël's famous disciple de Bonald proposed in 1805, or history and literature are *intertwined* or *interwoven,* as Marx and Engels would have it in their *German Ideology* of 1845; sometimes the literary work *corresponds* to social developments, as Marx suggested in his *Critique of Political Economy* (1859). Literature is seen as *bound up* with historical conditions; the periodization of Expressionism, for instance, closely follows the course of historical changes. Yet these posited connections remain largely undefined and free of specific economic data; I suspect that Hans Mayer largely operates within the tradition of German *Geistesgeschichte* disguised as political theory, and relies on dramatic rather than differentiated signals of those historical turning points which affect biographical, thematic, and formal elements in literature. I, for one, am not satisfied with the explanation that along with the construction of the Berlin Wall came a new literary obsession with current problems (an obsession which Mayer rightly considers oppressive); and the assurance that the new *Zeitgeist* literature is *connected with changes in economics and politics* strikes me as incomplete, as long as I am told very little about the exact nature of these changes and the precise mode of the connection. In practice it turns out that Hans Mayer (like Franz Mehring before him) often works with a technique of juxtaposition. The organization of his Fielding essay (1951) is characteristic of his early work: first a short sketch of English economic conditions, touching on the impoverishment of the small freeholders; then Fielding's biography, and, finally, the apodictic assertion that Fielding is a master of realism because his work reflects the proper historical circumstances. Hans Mayer proves more convincing in his stimulating essay on Balzac and his poet-figure Lucien de Rubempré (1952), channeling sociological material into a biographical approach, or in his close readings of some difficult poems by Bertolt Brecht, Peter Huchel, and Paul Celan, where he uses a dash of sociological information with the sensitivity of a true friend of literature. In his Balzac essay Mayer shows that the figure of Lucien enables the novelist to objectify the personal temptation posed by the artist's existence as drop-out from the normal economic world; and the private catharsis saves Balzac from any personal danger. The essay combines sociological terminology with a psychological approach and comes close to offering a spirited German counterpart to Edmund Wilson's interpretations of Dickens and Kipling.

Hans Mayer is a Marxist apologist for middle-class literature, and accordingly often finds himself forced to temper his enthusiasm with reservations and warnings; confronting the gates of Utopia, his favorite authors are heralds, predecessors, voices crying in the desert, prophets, and bridge-builders. Bourgeois art, Mayer emphasizes, is primarily the art of the novel; and from his basic assumption he proceeds with a series of impressive individual studies, from Johann Gottfried Schnabel (in whose prose we find German "lives" portrayed with a wealth of realistic detail) to Thomas Mann, who represents the end-phase of the German middle class and simultaneously transcends it.

In Mayer's analyses of the most recent novels, conservative tendencies make themselves more clearly felt; Mayer is more at home with traditional mimetic assumptions than with the self-willed narrator-subject of the *nouveau roman.* In his study of Max Frisch, Mayer tests the possibilities of reading *Stiller* either as a marriage novel or as a portrayal of metaphysical and existential problems, but concludes that the *social* element is the essential one: the true theme of the novel is life and literature in the age of technological reproduction. Compared to Stiller, Frisch's novel *Mein Name sei*

Gantenbein has only lesser virtures; all it can offer, Mayer suggests, is a *lukewarm sensation of story after story;* and the socially oriented critic refuses to recognize Frisch's sovereign aesthetic game as an artistic high point in his development. The same holds true for Heinrich Böll: Mayer respects him as a realistic critic of German provinciality, but at the same time he tries to hold him to a *petit bourgeois role;* he regards Böll's stylistic experiments of the later 1960s as problematic mistakes, born of Böll's permanent opposition to any kind of ideology. Mayer does have words of appreciation for his young Cologne compatriot, Jürgen Becker, and some of the younger writers, but he follows the experiments of the older and middle generation more with skepticism than with deep sympathy.

Mayer is a Protean critic, challenged to sensitive responses more by the culinary—not to say opulent—aspect of the arts than by abstract systematics. Lucien Goldmann's theoretical self-tortures are foreign to him; rather, he seeks *mutual influences between subjective creativity and objective social conditions,* or, in general outlines, *the social links,* and leaves the methodological bickering to others. His critical perceptivity saves him from radical historicism; unlike Goldmann, he does not see the work of art swallowed by the waves of history. Like Ernst Fischer and Karel Kosík, Mayer suggests that the historical moment of creation is transitory, and that the product created implies a message transcending the passing moment of creation; there is historicity, but also something more enduring. We are clearly reaching a turning point at which the traditional value-theory of Marxist literary criticism and the preceding German historicism are called sharply into question.

In the context of recent philosophical Marxism, the theoretical implications of Hans Mayer's criticism seem rather conservative, and curiously restricted to a recurring emphasis on an inescapable but vague connection between history and art and on the coming downfall of the bourgeois world. Yet as an untiring advocate of enlightenment and a spirited and quick-witted *homme de lettres,* Mayer has other virtues. Mayer may be heading the German department at the Hannover Technical University, but in his essays he moves gracefully throughout world literature, rather than keeping to German nooks, groves, and crannies. As a thirty-year-old refugee he intensified his literary scholarship with studies of Büchner, Bergson, Tolstoi, Rimbaud, and Poe, and the sixty-year-old master of world literature still does not tire of citing Ionesco, Gombrowicz, Pasternak, or Fernando Pessoa. Among his more recent works, Mayer's triptych on Sartre strikes me as especially interesting. Nothing could be farther from Mayer's intentions than to belittle Sartre's achievement on dogmatic grounds; he has difficulties in accepting Sartre's attempt to combine Marxist theory with other methodological approaches. Mayer fears that the class point of view is threatened by Sartre's *methodological syncretism.* It is a strange reproof to come from a critic who for many years has illuminated and provoked us with his admirably effective technique of balancing and combining the alternatives of close reading and historical analysis.

* * *

Ernst Fischer has changed a good deal in the course of his career as political thinker and literary critic. As Social Democratic newspaper editor, a commentator for Radio Moscow, Austrian Secretary of State for Education, and member of parliament, he has seriously and passionately searched for the elusive happiness of free Man through the left-wing Labyrinths of our time.

Ernst Fischer's literary essays of the nineteen-forties and early fifties combine conventional trains of Socialist Realist reasoning with sudden flashes of personal insight. We find a chained sensibility eager to demonstrate *realistic characterization and portrayal of the typical,* as demanded by the cultural policies of the Communist party. The most provocative essay of Fischer's earlier period is "Doctor Faustus and the German Cataclysm" (1949). He carefully investigates the political implications of Thomas Mann's novel, and his trenchant remarks reveal the customary apologetics produced by Leftist Mann-interpreters (including Lukács) as insubstantial *bellezza*-sociology. Fischer acknowledges Mann's undeniable artistic achievement, but he categorically refuses to credit the novel with any political relevance. He asserts that Mann's novel *corresponds to the romantic cravings of those many millions whose Germany had collapsed,* and since history appears in the novel as a *mythological tempest sweeping by,* Adrian Leverkuhn's story constitutes *a relapse into the worst kind of Romantic fate-tragedy (Schicksalstragödie);* social questions *go up in a smoke of psychology, mythology, and demonology.* Fischer claims that the concrete problems of Fascist power are dealt with *in a spiritual realm peopled by demons and ghosts,* and rightly feels uncomfortable at seeing the brutalities of German Fascism aestheticized into the tender portrayal of an avant-garde composer: of all the dubious metaphors for Fascism surely the most inappropriate.

In his critical studies *On the Necessity of Art* (published in Dresden in 1956 and three years later in English translation in London), Fischer advances his revision of aesthetic theories and norms. Still half-veiled in the terminology of prescribed "realism," his vision of art's history and function implies a forceful attack on the Marxist squares. Fischer still accepts the traditional "mirroring" function of art, but he now emphasizes that all art, in its essential capacity to reveal man's endless potentialities (an idea close to Ernst Bloch's concept of *Vorschein*), transcends the historical moment: Homer and Aeschylus reflect the conditions in a bygone slave society, but as revelations of human grandeur their works are more contemporary than ever. The triadic rhythm of Fischer's scheme is reminiscent of the religious assumptions of German Idealism (which usually distinguishes the stages of wholeness, fragmentation, and renewed paradise), but the accents are placed differently. In the long development of literature, the figure of the tribal magician shows the first traces of individuation; Greek sea-faring merchants introduce an even more radically subjective element, which finds its aesthetic expression in rejecting of the old forms of the tribal chronicle and the epic; and finally, capitalist society establishes itself in three "thrusts"—the Renaissance, the French Revolution, and the fateful year 1848, when alienation, impersonalization, and bureaucratization begin to triumph in full force. The resilient meaning of Romantic art and poetry resides in providing an answer to the vicissitudes of alienation and in seeking a world restored to new wholeness; it is an art that embodies a protest against the fragmentation of man and, according to Fischer, forms the essence of all subsequent realism—among the realists, therefore, we should prefer Stendhal to Balzac, who allied himself with the powers that be. In pursuing his discovery that Romantic art constitutes the true reply to alienation, Fischer formulates an explosive argument against Socialist Realism. He again distinguishes (as did Roman Jacobson before him) between realism as an ontological element of all art (for when has art *not* aspired to grasp human realities?) and a realistic mode of narration as developed at a specific moment in the historical past. Like Adorno, Fischer insists that insights into new realities call for new artistic methods: old forms of realism fail to capture new ways of living, and the necessary new "realism" (perhaps another name for the romantic opposition to any kind of alienation) may freely employ the most audacious and untried artistic strategies.

In the 1960s Fischer has completely broken with the

"cold" Marxism perpetuated by repressive governments, and he has been formulating a vision of the future centering on the spontaneous and whole human being. The result is a "third" position, which finds its hope among the productive intellectuals and restless students rather than among the "blockheads" in Moscow and Washington (or the unthinking, consumption-crazy proletariat). It is telling that Fischer discerns alienation and impersonalization not only in the capitalist countries but in the planned societies as well. Collective ownership of the means of production has apparently been unable to reconstitute man as a human being; and the coming reign of freedom will rest on the political spontaneity of the individual and on a scientifically sober attitude toward one's daily work.

These projections of a future society directly lead to Fischer's interpretation of Franz Kafka, which (to be sure) relies more heavily on biographical data than on the occasional readings of the texts. Kafka, like his predecessor Heinrich von Kleist, is seen as a Columbus of alienation: Kafka's personal isolation in the midst of peoples, religions, and languages corresponds to man's social situation in industrial society and enables him forcefully to define isolation, impersonalization, and bureaucratization. But Fischer says Kafka and means modern world literature. The realistic novel recedes into history, and the Marxist reader may finally turn to experimental writing again—to Paul Celan, Wolf Biermann, Erich Fried, Hans Magnus Enzensberger, Salinger's *Catcher in the Rye,* and even the *nouveau roman,* which, however, offers little historical insight.

Fischer's development as a literary critic reflects more than mere changes in his attitude towards forms of government or toward George Lukács; it reflects transformations in the very process of critical evaluation. As long as Fischer subscribed to the traditional mirror theory, literary significance implied re-presentation of historical conditions; thus, Grillparzer's childhood reflected the old monarchy, and his life was to be interpreted as an image of a transitional epoch of Austrian history. As soon as the critic relinquishes the mirror theory, the process of evaluation changes too: freed from the burdens of representation, those writers acquire new significance who most sensitively experience the universal alienation of man within their private world and who articulate their experience in a work of art. *Archetypal* experience (*Urerlebnis*) comes close to being Fischer's new favorite methodological term. As literary critic Fischer has become a belated ally of Wilhelm Dilthey; and the ideas of experience and poetry, *Erlebnis* and *Dichtung,* are enjoying their left-wing renaissance in his visionary version.

* * *

Lucien Goldmann thinks in terms of totalities, comprehensive tendencies, representative figures. Like Hans Mayer, he began as a student of law and, while still in his native Rumania, turned to dialectical materialism. During his subsequent exile in Prague and Zurich (where he wrote his doctoral dissertation on Kant), he devoted himself to history, sociology, and philosophy. As the present director of studies at the Ecole des Hautes Etudes, he works at constituting a synthesis of nineteenth-century French positivist scholarship with his own late-Hegelian speculative passion.

Goldmann elaborates general descriptions of social groups in their reactions to the historical changes which they must confront, and the characteristic thoughts and linguistic constructs by which they respond. As cultural critic, Goldmann attempts to define the relationship between group consciousness and the work of art: a given group (in his earlier works identical with a social caste or class) evolves certain expectations and ideas which distinguish it from other groups; and the group consciousness which Goldmann calls *vision du monde* (echoing Dilthey's *Weltanschauung*) crystallizes in philosophical systems or in the writer's fictive world. Goldmann's investigations seek to define that relationship between group consciousness and work of art which he terms "homology," i.e. the historical correlation between a diffuse *vision du monde* and an articulate philosophy or work of art in which firm thought content (*contenu*) prevails, determining and organizing the form. Pascal's paradoxes and Racine's tragedies correspond to the Jansenists' aversion to absolute monarchy; Kant's tragic philosophy derives from the despair of the German middle classes condemned to inactivity by actual political circumstances; and the recent intellectual changes of the French Left are reflected, novel by novel, in the writings of Malraux. Diffuse group awareness finds articulate form in individual works, or a clear and well-organized *contenu.*

The trouble is that Goldmann's scheme gives little chance to the productive individual who succeeds in unifying and articulating the scattered elements of a *Weltanschauung;* the individual poet matters only insofar as he identifies to the highest degree with fundamental trends and becomes, whether he minds or not, the spokesman of a group. A Hegelian mistrust of the individual made prominent only by the cunning group-consciousness informs Goldmann's recurrent polemics against the biographical positivism practiced at the Sorbonne and against the (subjective) deviations of psychology. Goldmann rightly objects that every biographical and factual detail should first be examined for its function; and it is certainly a dubious proposition to reconstruct from anecdotal material the psychology of authors long dead. Goldmann has more serious methodological objections to Freud. In concentrating on the individual's subconscious, Freud is choosing the wrong subject: the socially committed critic is to consider the individual only a partial element of a more inclusive "subject" consisting of the web of interpersonal relationships within the group.

When discussing Goldmann as a literary critic, I am inclined to separate his important study *Le dieu caché* (1955) from his works on the literary sociology of the novel and on Genêt; in these later studies a working hypothesis unfortunately hardens into a rigid scheme, or traditional determinism in new dress. Goldmann's *Le dieu caché,* as significant in the development of Marxist criticism as Franz Mehring's *Lessing-Legende* of 1893, demonstrates the usefulness of "homology" as a tool of criticism. Goldmann carefully analyzes the clash of complex interests of many French aristocrats and parliamentary lawyers (*officiers*) with the rapidly consolidating absolute monarchy and its administrative representatives (*commissairs*) in the late thirties of the seventeenth century, and discloses a group orientation towards withdrawal from the world, asceticism, and pessimism; Pascal's paradoxes and Racine's tragedies articulate a historical state of mind. But in Goldmann's *Pour une sociologie du roman* (1965) a scheme which originated in Lukács's *Theorie des Romans* (1920) wins out, and "trends" prove more important than the works of art which are totally submerged in the streams of history. In his theory of the novel, Goldmann puts Lukács's early idealism to his own use: Lukács had explained the novel as the biography of a problematical hero searching, like Novalis, for essence (*Wesentlichkeit*) in a fragmented world, and in Goldmann's variation this hero of old challenges the capitalist world of "market value" (*valeur d'échange*) in hopes of finding the original Arcadian "use value" of things (*valeur d'usage*)—neither Goldmann nor Lukács answers the question as to why this paradigmatic hero of the German *Entwicklungsroman* stubbornly prefers to absent himself from the Anglo-American tradition, from Jane Austen, Thackeray, George Eliot, or Henry James. Goldmann's scheme of the developing European novel prefers the rigid to the unforeseen. In the period of economic liberalism (1800-1890), the individual interests of the hero (for instance, in Balzac's novels of bourgeois society) had their relevance; in the period of capitalist monopolism (1890-1914), marked by cutthroat competition of trusts and nations, the suppression of the individual commences, and finds expression in the novels of Musil, Kafka and, in a delayed reaction, Nathalie Sarraute. In our own time of economic "interventionism" capitalists have learned to avoid crises and to organize the internal consumer market; and inevitably we are witnessing the triumph of *l'univers réifié des objets* and with it the *nouveau roman* of Robbe-Grillet, in which the heroes have disappeared completely, leaving only things. The scheme is all the tidier since it excludes the potentially contrary evidence provided by the contemporary British and American novel.

Goldmann's theory of culture and his practical criticism often diverge remarkably. Goldmann's theory of culture offers new, subtle, and often surprising insights, but his interpretations of literary texts often fall back upon nineteenth-century techniques. Goldmann has trouble overcoming the retarding effect of an implied mirror theory (however indirect) and preventing his concrete readings of individual novels or dramas from disintegrating into a series of scene summaries or mere illustrative quotations intended to show how fictional characters embody changing collective awareness or historical currents; Goldmann's only technical literary analysis (in his recent study of Genêt's stage directions) was of fragmentary success. Despite a wealth of material, Goldmann's discussion of André Malraux demonstrates his old-fashioned, if not antiquated, method of interpretation. He analyzes Malraux's novels in chronological order from *Les conquérants* (1927) to *Les Noyers de l'Altenburg* (1943) and tries to show that Malraux's intellectual development runs parallel *avec l'ensemble* (a favorite expression of Taine's) of contemporary ideological transformations. Malraux's literary course represents a general trend among the French Left *entre deux guerres* to replace Marxist orientation by an ahistorical, metaphysical idea of man. In his individual analyses Goldmann again concentrates on scenes and characters; he explains that certain characters incarnate the revolutionary forces, distinguishes three types, which correspond in turn to three possibilities of revolutionary behavior, and seeks to support his characterizations by examining important plot episodes. Only once does he discuss a matter of language (the repetition of an image), and it is difficult to guess where or how the interpreter Goldmann wishes to transcend the tried-and-true nineteenth-century tradition of literary analysis in terms of representative types.

But I do not doubt Goldmann's literary sensitivity; his early essay on Karl Kraus (1945), written long before he formulated his systematic theory of culture, offers a convincing and fertile combination of sociological and literary insight. Kraus emerges as *le grand réactionnaire,* who looks into a future without a future and lovingly uses language as his ultimate weapon in a lonely and uncompromising battle for the best bourgeois ideas of the past. In this brief essay Goldmann perhaps does Franz Werfel and Alfred Kerr some injustice, but his sharp portrait of the bitter satirist is nothing short of unforgettable.

* * *

Marxist literary critics (to approach a conclusion) have increasingly turned against the traditional idea of art as a mirror of society massively employed by Lukács and by the Communist *otrazhenie* theoreticians. Goldmann, who clings most closely to young Lukács, has particular difficulty in extracting himself from the restrictive implications of the traditional idea ultimately derived from Plato's ironic attack against the all-too-flexible artists: his concept of "homology" between group consciousness and coherent *contenu* does not really constitute a radical departure from reflection theory; and Roland Barthes has reason for being skeptical. Hans Mayer avoids an unalterable position, and whereas in his Leipzig period he occasionally stressed the mirroring function of art, in his most recent essays he concentrates on implying a theory of links, which offers him the (often vague) privilege of connecting the most diverse political elements with different texts and trends in literature. Ernst Fischer has come to break decisively with the theory of reflection. He relied on it in Moscow, but in the 1950s he began to argue that art had a dual function (to mirror and to explore), and in the sixties he resolved to reject the mirror metaphor completely and to consider art as a means for probing and bringing to light the full range of human possibilities.

But in the political context of contemporary Marxism, any more or less articulate opposition to the mirror theory constitutes an eminently political act of resistance against the doctrine of Socialist Realism and Neo-Stalinism. Challenging the mirror metaphor inevitably implies challenging the new orthodoxy and siding with those groups which are trying to reconstitute Marxism as humanism, free of police terror, and compulsion; and it is characteristic that the revolt against Socialist Realism expresses itself in the new vocabulary of alienation and the enthusiasm for romantic and modern experimental art.

Yet recent Marxist critics are far from unified in their views: in aesthetic matters, Hans Mayer inclines to an enlightened traditionalism; and Lucien Goldmann calls himself an *antiformalist* who deals with the literary innovation of the *nouveau roman* in order to discover correspondences to contemporary depersonalization and reification. Fischer alone has radically broken with the classicist and realist traditions of Marxist literary criticism: his distinction between realism as an ontological stance and as a temporary phenomenon of literature combines with his enthusiasm for new art and has a strong attraction for young intellectuals in Prague, Leipzig, Belgrade, and elsewhere. Fischer does not hesitate to take a long hard look at his own past, does not defend (as does Goldmann) Stalin's pact with Hitler as a historical necessity, and commands strong sympathy from those young socialist critics who themselves have grown up under rigid Communist systems.

But even modern Marxist criticism still bears the burden of historicism that Marxism inherited from German intellectual developments. Tense historicity impairs present value judgments: if a work of art is exclusively meaningful because it reflects the class conflicts of 1789 or 1848, we have trouble finding any convincing reason why it should appeal to our sensibilities today; and Marx himself was rightly perplexed by (and tried in vain to answer) the question as to why Greek art, the product of a bygone age of slavery, remained meaningful to him on August 23, 1857. Goldmann seems least concerned with art's surviving its moment of homology; Hans Mayer at least confirms Karel Kosík's suggestion that it might be useful to distinguish between the historical aspect and the durance (*Dauer*) of a literary test; and Ernst Fischer, again far bolder than his colleagues, postulates a new resilience of art as more than mere historical exploration of man. But it seems to me that Marxist literary criticism, even of the most recent and daring brand, has rarely ventured to confront another problem. In his *Economic and Philosophic Manuscripts* (1844), young Marx distinguishes between the evil, brutal, and greedy age of "having" and that blissful reign of freedom when man is to be purified of all possessive urges; and I feel that much of Marxist criticism in its own way still partakes of the age of "having" which it is supposed to transform. The critics who appropriate, if not manipulate, a text for their own purposes discover precursors and allies in distant figures of literary history and deny, to the aesthetic monuments of the past, their own way of life, closely resemble that greedy mineral merchant, who, according to the young Marx, knows only the commercial value of the mineral and not *seine eigentliche Natur,* its particular mode of being. It is the acquisitive, the possessive urge within the Marxist critic, old and new, that is his—and our—most inveterate antagonist.

YALE UNIVERSITY

FRENCH FORMALISM

Michael Riffaterre

A New Criticism has been developing in France—mostly in the sixties—led by a group of young writers centered around Roland Barthes. Each of these is as intensely preoccupied with criticism and literary theory as with his own practice of literature: poets like Marcelin Pleynet and Denis Roche; novelists like Philippe Sollers, Jean Ricardou, and Jean Thibaudeau; philosophers like Sollers' wife, Julia Kristeva.[1] Their ideas find expression mainly in the periodical *Tel Quel*.[2]

The theoretical views of this group have been deeply influenced by, sometimes borrowed from, and often rationalized with the help of, the Russian Formalists. For that reason I shall call them French Formalists.[3] We could call them structuralists (as a matter of fact, by replacing *structuralism*, a descriptive term, with *formalism*, which belongs to the language of history, and perhaps polemics, I am reversing what the Prague Linguistic Circle did when it reformulated Russian formalism).[4] Their approach is based upon the analysis of structures; but then the term *structuralist* would include the style analysts who pay close attention to the way things are said, that is, to the variants in which structures manifest themselves.[5] Our Formalists prefer to make straight for the invariants hidden beneath the variants, to start from *a priori* models which they later verify by the texts, rather than to build their models from textual data. The term *structuralist*, again, is used of marginal Marxist criticism, such as Lucien Goldmann's: the written work of art is the literary expression of social structures, of concepts shaped by historical and economic circumstances. Such an approach postulates a causal relationship between the inner structure of the work of art, and external factors, the social structures. Whereas the fundamental tenet of our Formalists is immanent analysis, the study of a system of functions entirely within the text.[6]

As I have remarked, these views are an extension of linguistic analysis to literary language, pioneered in the Russia of the twenties: a basic reference work of the French group is *Théorie de la littérature,* a translation by Tzv. Todorov from Russian formalists of that period.[7] Seminal also are the works of Roman Jakobson, one of the surviving Russian formalists. Several of his essays on poetics have appeared in French translation in book form;[8] together with Cl. Lévi-Strauss he wrote one of the first formalist analyses of a French poem, in 1962.[9] Since then more translations of his work have appeared in *Tel Quel*.[10] Prominent among the ideas of Jakobson adopted by his French disciples are the concept of the poetic function of language (and its correlation with the referential function),[11] and the difference he draws between a metaphoric and a metonymic relation among textual components, upon which is based his definition of poetic language and his attempt to define literary realism.

The most influential of the essays included in *Théorie de la littérature,* so far, have been the contributions of V. Propp on the structures of folk tales, and of V. Shklovskij on the typology of narrative prose. These have inspired the activities of scholars such as A. J. Greimas[12] at the Ecole pratique des Hautes Etudes (a perennial seat of subversive scholarship hidden away in the recesses of the Sorbonne, the University being closed to ideas of this kind). A more public spokesman, again, is Roland Barthes.[13] Kristeva is another link with Russian formalism; she introduced to a French audience the ideas of Russian semiotics specialists and Bakhtin's works on Dostoevskij and Rabelais. In essence, Mikhail Bakhtin tried to do for the novel what Propp (and Skaftymov) had done for oral literature.[14]

An effort is being made to extend the application of syntax to verbal units larger than the sentence. Since sentence boundaries are the outer limits of linguistics, the aim is thus to create a linguistics of larger units, such as the *narrative,*[15] the *description* (not to be confused with the traditional genres); this new discipline should be capable of ultimately embracing the entire structural ensemble of a text, poem, novel, or whatever.

The fundamental principle here is that a literary text is a finite combinatory system of signs within the combinatory system of language. Any explanation of the text, and, finally, any judgment of it, must therefore be arrived at through a description of its structures. The discrete components of a text cannot be defined or understood separately, but only through identification of their correlates and definition of the functional relationships between correlates. The meaning of the components depends upon their distribution in the ensemble.

The literary text is thus approached exactly the way structural anthropology approaches myth, and there is no doubt that literary formalism would have arrived in France later and less conspicuously but for the present popularity of Cl. Lévi-Strauss. He starts, after all, from the premise that social forms are a language, that the myth is articulated as a language. But French interest in formalism can be traced further back: as René Wellek puts it, Paul Valéry is the poet who moved "poetry completely out of history into the realm of the absolute," and saw it as a closed microcosm, where form is words in pattern, where content is what he calls an impure form, a mixed form.[16] Valéry, again, drew the line between the author and his work, between the genesis and the end product. Valéry was the first in France to discredit intention as a critical criterion. In a way, French formalism simply systematizes Valéry's ideas,[17] with the help of a rather superficial terminology borrowed mostly from Jakobson.[18]

The French formalists' importance lies not in any originality of theory. It lies first in the impact they are having upon the history of French criticism and upon the French idea of literature; and second, in the implications of their *practice* of criticism for the future of literary analysis. I shall not dwell much on this first point. The group is apt to shift ideological positions suddenly, with accompanying excommunications of this member or that. These shifts are not always purely intellectually motivated, and any account of them must soon be outdated. It is upon the second point that I shall insist: it raises questions that will remain valid when the quarrels and vicissitudes of any particular Movement are in the past.

First, their historical impact: for Americans, accustomed to the New Criticism, it is hard to imagine the violence of the controversy that has been raging between the *Tel Quel* team and the literary Establishment.[19] For one thing, the structuralist approach is diametrically opposed to the positivistic, historicist approach of traditional criticism. That criticism explains a work of art by factors external to it: previous works that may have influenced it or are comparable to it; the author's life, his psychology, expecially his psychopathology; historical circumstances. Even freshly fertilized with psychoanalysis or Marxism, this criticism remains in fact *an aesthetics of exterior motivations:*[20] it accounts for the components of a text in terms of filiation, of temporal determinism. Formalism, on the contrary, sees the work of art as an absolute, defines its components in terms of inter-relations, of spatial determinism,[21] and finds their meaning in their functions.

This total opposition would not *per se* explain the passions aroused: traditional criticism treats Barthes and his followers as heretics and regards their approach as a threat to French values.[22] This bitterness flows from the consequences, for the critic, of conceiving of the work of art as an autonomous system of structures, i.e. independent of the referential functions of language. Literature, it appears, neither expresses the author's personality nor represents reality: it is a quite arbitrary exercise, it is no more than a system of signs, and its essence lies not in a "message" but in that system. So that criticism can no longer speak of mimetic faithfulness of texts to reality, of the moral conformity or propriety of a message. It can no longer base its value judgments upon the truth of the work of art, but only upon its *validity*—that is, *the coherence of its inner system.* Such an ontological assertion of the literature's *literariness*[23] must necessarily produce a polemical or even revolutionary attitude. For it entails the elimination of any criticism that still postulates an expressive and representational literature. All such criticism is condemned, as is that very conception of literature, as the product of the ideology, as the ethical model,[24] of a given stage in social evolution: hopelessly passé. The formalists have no trouble demonstrating that the pseudo-factual and pseudo-objective tenets of French University criticism are founded upon the taboos of taste and morals inherited from French Classicism; that the allegedly universal values of criticism—such as stylistic *clarity* (the famous *clarté française*)—merely reflect the values of the classes in power during the seventeenth century.[25] The fierce reaction to these views would seem to prove that the taboos of the French Establishment, rather than objective principles, are indeed at stake.

French formalists make it a point to speak of *texts* rather than of *literature*. They have lately become obsessed with the implications that the analysis of verbal structures must have for the study, and possible transformation, of social structures—which are, after all, systems of signs themselves. Hence the *Théorie d'ensemble* recently published in an effort to keep tabs on their own evolution: it reflects a closer and closer identification with Marxist Leninism.[26] This is a development that strikingly parallels the evolution of their predecessors, the Russians, and also the French Surrealists.[27]

But now to a consideration of how they practice criticism. The French formalists' insistence upon the referential autonomy of literary verbal structures is correct from the linguistic viewpoint, but it still needs considerable refinement before it can be of much use in critical practice.

For one thing, it is most easily applied to literary works that were consciously intended as non-expressive and non-representational: a page in such a work has only this to say: *I am literature* (a formula I borrow from Valéry); the kind of poetry, for instance, that Valéry dreamt of, "where the transformation of thoughts into other thoughts would look more important than any thought, where the interplay between figures of speech would be the real subject."[28] Hence the formalists' approval of poets like Mallarmé, of prose writers like Lautréamont and Raymond Roussel; hence their interest in works that are meditations upon·projected poems, rather than poems in the ordinary sense of the word—texts that reflect their own image like a mirror, like Ponge's *Sur Malherbe;*[29] Hence the inchoate or projective nature of the formalists' own novels and essays, which are their own metalanguage. Paradoxically, then, their literature is in this respect

just as dated as the literature of the criticism they reject.[30]
In a comparable phase, Russian formalism was at first closely
associated with the Futurist poets.[31]

But even when they deal with a literature that so well suits
their theoretical preoccupations, and still more, of course,
when they turn to other forms of writing and to other
periods, the concept of referential autonomy blinds them to
the modes of reader-perception of the literary message: for
example, though poetry focuses upon words rather than
upon things, the reader, conditioned by the constant use of
referential language, *rationalizes as if there were a reference.*
He is like Alice listening to *Jabberwocky:* obviously she
cannot understand, but still she has a feeling that any minute
she will be able to. Hence the oneiric or fantastic rationalizations so frequent when we read nonsense poetry or
automatic-writing poetry. The mechanism of this *presumption of reference* is just as central to the literary phenomenon
as the absence of reference that triggers it. The problem
remains unexplored.

A fortiori, when formalist criticism treats of texts that
were composed within the frame of an expressive, mimetic
aesthetics (most of literature), this mechanism is everything.
To study the inner structure alone is clearly insufficient;
criticism must open out upon the whole domain of anthropology. Not because of any political or sociological bias
(although the group does lean in that direction), but because
the text *looks* like a reference to things. The techniques of
verisimilitude, for example, and perhaps all the devices of the
mimesis of reality, can be described as references to a set of
verbal references to majority opinions, popular wisdom,
etc.—in short, the corpus of associations that a text may
trigger in the reader's mind, all the commonplaces that define
the mythology of an era.

The problem of the *connotations* (secondary meanings)
which signs take on because they have been steeped in such

mythologies and are interpreted in the context of such mythologies, inspired R. Barthes to develop his *sémiologie* (not *semiotics,* the study of signs, of which linguistics form a part, but *semiology,* conceived as part of linguistics). This discipline studies the connotations that any sign (verbal sign or non-verbal symbol) takes on from serving its function in a system of conventions (be it the context, or metalanguage, or a rhetoric). For example, signs used at the level Barthes calls *écriture* (between the linguistic and stylistic levels), that is, signs used as markers of *genre* or indices of the aesthetics (realist, etc.) chosen by the writer.

The difficulty French formalists run into, it seems to me, is that their selection of a structural model to be applied to the text often amounts to a selection of a mythology different from that of the text. For instance, Barthes's choice of a psychoanalytical model to describe Racine is tantamount to relating the seventeenth-century text to a prehistoric mythology. [32] This is defended as a means of exploring the potentialities of the text, and more especially as a method that yields a modern reading of the text—a reading geared to our own interests. [33] Unfortunately, it threatens our understanding of the text as style, and so threatens formalism itself. For the mythology that regulates the mimetic system of the text is exterior to it *only* from the viewpoint of genetic criticism (from such a viewpoint, that mythology is a cause of the text, or one of the elements that conditioned its composition). From the viewpoint of form, it seems to me, *this mythology is encoded* in the style—in the shape of clichés, for example, of cliché renewals, of cultural allusions (quotations, etc.), and more importantly, in the shape of associative word sequences that mold sentences as often or more often, I believe, than the non-lexical narrative or descriptive structures studied so far by the formalists. [34]

This encoded mythology must be properly decoded; if you substitute for it another mythology, your whole interpretation goes wrong. This is what happens when Jean Ricardou tries to show that E. A. Poe's *Gold-Bug,* like a poem, has more than one level of signification. The story is told as a narrative, at the "denotative" level, but is repeated by symbols at the "connotative" level. Certain details, pointless at first blush, take on meaning because the narrative structure correlates them with significant features of the tale. No later than the third line of the text, the protagonist is presented to us as the scion of an old Huguenot family of New Orleans. According to Ricardou, this would be *per se* a pointless detail, but in the context of the story that follows it is not pointless. In that context, the protagonist's religion—with its emphases upon Scripture reading by the individual—makes him a privileged, predestined reader, decipherer par excellence of the cryptogram that is to lead him to Captain Kidd's buried treasure.[35] Alas, this is not only farfetched, it is unimaginable except from the French viewpoint of a French reader—and hardly then. In French mythology there is a definitive opposition between Protestants and Roman Catholics. This opposition is learned in the French high school; history teachers attribute the Renaissance to (among other causes) the Protestant return to the holy texts, the new birth of curiosity in the Scriptures. The word *Protestant* may have some such connotation for the American reader too, but it is not what he thinks of first—if only because Protestants are in the majority here. The opposition would not occur to American Catholics—or if it did, it would be seen from the Roman standpoint and there would be no connotation of Protestant superiority. For the American reader, the only *Huguenot* connotation here is oriented by the opposition *Huguenot / non-Hugenot Protestant,* which is a social connotation: its sole purpose is to give this particular character membership in the aristocracy of First Settler descendants. It endows him with more substance, it anchors him in reality.[36]

We might go further and look upon it as part of a narrative

101

structure: it sets up more firmly one pole of a basic dramatic opposition, *former wealth / present poverty,* in itself a variant of *past glory / present decay.* The situation is pregnant with the possibility—nay, the imminence—that the Wheel of Fate is about to take another turn. What has fallen shall rise again. The destitute hero is thus unmistakably foreordained to redress the wrongs of Destiny by discovering the treasure (popular stories and folklore are filled with penniless sons of great families finding and recovering the lost wealth of their ancestors).[37]

So that even if a text is not a mimesis of reality, it is still the mimesis of a verbal mythology. But not just any reader's mythology will do as a referent. The text calls for an ideal reading attitude; its score, so to speak, indicates the cultural context within which it must be deciphered.

A second consequence of the formalist idea that the text is an autonomous system of meanings (the first being the radical modification of the concept of mimesis) is that the author is done away with.[38] The belief that the poem expresses the personality of the author, as an effect expresses a cause, is now seen as outdated: it is the ideology of nineteenth-century Romanticism. To offer the author as an explanation for the work of art would be psychologism, or geneticism. In truth, this attitude does save the critic much unverifiable hypothesizing. It also rids criticism of one of its main obstacles to a genuine understanding of what makes a poem unique: generalizations based upon what we think we know about the workings of the human mind. But it does raise the problem of how to replace the intersubjective approach[39] — that is to say, criticism as defined and practiced by Georges Poulet: the intersubjective critic must feel over again, think over again, imagine over again, re-live from inside the emotions, the thoughts, the imaginings of the author.[40] Inner re-creation, with all the dangers that subjectivity and mystical intuition entail; ideally, the critic's understanding will irradiate the poem from that very center where the author once spun his web. The formalists reply with a grid, instead of a web: they set up a model of relationships that should account (in the critic's metalanguage) for the distribution and interactions of the components of the text (of the object language, that is, the author's). Such a grid will inevitably be so complex as to be unique: thus it fulfills the purpose of criticism, which is to find out the uniqueness of a text. There is no preconceived, unchangeable grid, there is what Barthes calls *parametric criticism:* [41] the metalanguage changes with the texts under study. In order for the metalanguage to be imposed upon the object language, the former must be a system whose structure is isomorphic or analogous to the structure of the latter (that is, the poem). [42] The critic's choice of metalanguage he will use (be it sociological, psychoanalytical, aesthetic, or whatever) is up to him. In the eyes of the formalist, at least, this freedom is not license to say just anything he pleases about the text. It means merely that the code selected by the critic will not distort the object language so long as isomorphism is assured. [43] And this in turn depends upon the coherence of the structural system chosen, [44] and upon the exhaustiveness of the description (the metalanguage must saturate the object language: since it is a grammar of that language, it must account for every possible sentence in the text, and for the distribution of every textual component [45]). If the text resists, the arrangement of structures must be modified until total relevance is achieved. [46]

As may be well imagined, this is where their adversaries pounce upon the formalists. The latter are accused of that sin precisely: ignoring the resistance of the text, that is, disrespecting its letter whenever it happens to contradict their model. The formalists retort that those who believe a word has but one meaning—the right one, dictated by usage and the context—are not facing fact; they are picking out a reading method that corresponds not to the reality of the text, but to an ideology of aesthetic immobilism,[47] inherited from French Classicism in its narrowest sense—Boileau's sense—and kept alive by purist tradition—by Flaubert, for instance, in his critique of his own style. Genuine literality— respect for the text, period, not for the text seen through ideological lenses—should presuppose not monosemy but polysemy. It should assume the *coexistence of meanings for each significant unit.* To read faithfully is therefore to be aware of the *symbolism* of the signs the text is made of,[48] to make a complete discovery of the concurrent meanings of a word. I should say there are three such concurrent meanings: 1) the meaning in language, in the common code; 2) the restrictions imposed upon that meaning by the context, by the special code; and 3) above all, the *structural* meaning, the meaning in the system underlying the text, the meaning the word takes on by actualizing a structure. This French defini- tion of symbolism is borrowed straight from the Russian formalists and reflects, more expecially, the teachings of Jakobson. It certainly comes closest to defining what makes a literary text literary—its literariness as distinguished from the nature of verbal sequence used merely for communication.[49] And it certainly represents an important enrichment of the close reading methods so long practiced in France with an eye to strict literality alone.

It must be remarked, however, that the practical results achieved so far by the application of this theory remain uneven. And application is the ultimate proof. Discrepancies between the structural models proposed by the critics and the data supplied by the text occur with a frequency that we must try to explain.

Whether the analyst finds too much or too little in the text cannot be explained away as the accidental result of subjec- tive bias or of insufficient self-criticism. There is always an element of subjectivity in the first selection of a structural model; the resistance of the text should eliminate this subjectivity when the model is tried out. I suggest, then, that the fault lies in a failure of attention to an essential condition of the actual literary phenomenon, that is, the contact between text and reader: the condition of *perceptibility.* Perceptibility, in fact, seems to be the only important element of Russian formalist theory that French formalism has not explicitly adopted, possibly because of its initial relationship with Shklovskij's concept of deviation from the norm (*priëm ostrannenija*—literally, "device for making it strange") as the main characteristic of literary representation. [50] This idea has been rejected by Jakobson and others (including me), though for different reasons.

In any event, the nature of the perceptibility of the components of a text by its reader must be clarified if formalism is to avoid such pitfalls as finding hidden features in the text that are actually not hidden but nonexistent. Jean Ricardou, again, in his commentary on *The Gold-Bug,* assumes that the obsession with gold, and the imminence of treasure-finding, will be expressed on other levels than the semantic: he finds the word *gold* symbolically concealed in the spelling of other words. According to him, *Golconda* was the name Poe chose for the fabled land of riches, not *Eldorado,* because *Golconda* contains the letters of *gold* in their proper order! No one is likely to fall for this, especially since Poe himself wrote a poem on the land of golden dreams entitled *Eldorado.* Worse yet, Ricardou goes on to venture the proposition that "while reading it we cannot understand *god,* or its anacyclic *dog,* without emphasizing the surrounding *l's,* to wit, *good God, settled,* and, naturally inverted, *the violent howlings of the dog.*" He finds his gold again in groups like *right holding,* [51] etc. Needless to say, no reading is going to unearth *gold* in words where its graphic components are scattered, phonetically unstressed, sometimes even unpronounced. If any effect is to be achieved here, and any reader consensus, there will have to be at least some repetition to give the letters an exceptional group status in the sentence. Without any clue of this kind, the letters may have their role on the language level, but they remain absolutely unnoticeable, and therefore nonexistent on the level of style. Consequently they cannot form part of a structure and exercise a function in it. Here is another principle the formalists have failed to recognize: structures and functions are not to be observed only in the text; they must be observed, so to say, within the reader himself. If he has no way of perceiving them, hence no way of experiencing them, they may be linguistic features of the text, but they are not textual (or literary) features.[52]

As we see from Ricardou's analysis of Poe, French formalists seem to labor under the belief that every linguistic component of a literary text is equally and totally visible at the signifier's level.[53] This is, in my opinion, a hasty or superficial judgment upon the way the poetic function of language works (by poetic function is meant, of course, the orientation of the act of communication toward the form of the message[54]). It would be more accurate to speak of maximum or higher control exercised by the text over the reader's decoding: the text must contain formal variations that emphasize certain features by contrast with others and impose them, as anomalous in context, upon the reader's attention. If it were otherwise, everything in a text would be stressed, a contradiction in terms; an infinity of readings would be possible, which is not the case. This control must needs extend to ambiguities and polysemy: that a word is susceptible of several meanings is not enough to make it symbolic. The plurality must be actualized in context, so that the reader cannot escape it. It does not suffice to say a context is so built as to impose one particular meaning at a certain point or to tolerate more than one meaning at that point. We must say that in the second case it imposes more than one meaning, or forces the reader to entertain the possibility of a different reading.

It is because they disregard this principle that Philippe Sollers and Mercelin Pleynet discover far too many things in the name of one of the Marquis de Sade's characters. She is Clairwil, *the* corrupt woman in Sade's *Juliette.* Sollers declares that *Clairwil* should be read *clear will,* because Juliette learns vice and sin under her firm, enlightened guidance. Not so, retorts Pleynet, the name must be read *claire vile,* luminous and vile; this symbolizes the conflict between good and evil, human duality.[55] Sollers' reading, of course, is all cockeyed. Pleynet's is unacceptable because Sade explicitly condemns self-contradictory compounds ("it is impossible to coin a compound neologism made of two antithetical terms, because it would not be possible to understand it"[56]). But the point is that this controversy is idle, since the name does not permit such a multiple reading in the first place: it is simply shaped to look aristocratic, and British, which is twice as aristocratic. *Clair,* frequent enough in the names of the aristocracy, is a nobility marker. *Wil,* of course, is the exotic marker.[57] Hence the contrastive potential of deeper, completer degradation, the beautiful, noble lady brought low indeed: this is a commonplace of erotic thematology. The analysts' attention was attracted by a name made striking by its foreign spelling. But this perceptibility affects one meaning only—the socially symbolic. It does not actualize the polysemy of the name's components. In context the name remains unambiguous. The only reason Sollers and Pleynet overreacted to it is that they had read excepts from the Russian formalist B. V. Tomaševskij wherein he explains that the names of characters in Russian comedies often have satiric meanings. The rule does not apply here.[58]

Our conclusion must be that no element of a text can actualize a structure if that element is not forced selectively upon the reader's perception. In other words, no linguistic unit can have a structural function if it is not also a stylistic unit.

We must consider further the implications of perceptibility for the concept of latency (as formalists use the term in speaking of *latent structures*). Let us take an analysis of Barthes's as an example. Whenever intersubjectivity gets in his way, he is prone to discover in the text some structure that actually exists only in his own mind or is really an archetype—in any case is outside of the text. For instance, in a brilliant essay on the Roman historian Tacitus, he considers the latter's account of numerous political murders perpetrated on orders of the Roman emperors. Barthes tries to determine what structures give these narratives what he calls their "apocalyptic poetry." This leads him to view a group of synonymous episodes as so many variants of the same structure—that is, the *innocent tools* ("les outils innocents") which in each scene give its character to the climactic description of the actual assassination:

> Death is *praxis, techne,* its ways are instrumental. Dagger, sword, noose, eraser-knife for cutting veins, poison pen, oar or club for bludgeoning, blankets for smothering, rock for pushing off of, ceiling loaded with lead to crash down on its victim. . . . Death always comes with the help of the soft stuff ("la douce matiére") of life—wood, metal, fabric, innocent tools. . . . This world of terror needs no scaffold: . . . in an instant things change their calling, they lend themselves to Death.[59]

This is indeed a theme that makes its appearance in various literatures: the *innocent tools of evil.* In French literature I could cite Victor Hugo. He makes a tree complain that although it does not mind being cut down to be turned into a ship's mast, or the beam of a sheltering roof, it *does* resent being used as a gallows. In another of his poems, molten bronze turns red at the thought of being cast in the shape of a tyrant's statue.[60] If I were to put this in structural terms, I should say that the structure upon which the theme is founded consists in the transformation of an opposition: the opposition *innocence / evil* becomes *criminal innocence* in its active form, *sullied innocence* in its passive form. As Barthes explains matters, this structure is superimposed upon an animistic theme which is also based upon the transformation of an *animate / inanimate* opposition into *animated inanimate:* objects, things are endowed with a secret will of their own.

Unfortunately, these structures are not in Tacitus' text. First, the tools of death are never considered separate and apart from the human murderers who use them; there is no animism. Second, and most important, there is no innocence in a dagger, a sword, a noose: they are all professional killers. There is no softness in a rock. And certainly the ceiling loaded with lead to crush the Empress Agrippina may be called a mean character. The curious thing is that Barthes brings in the same structures a propos the tools used by common murderers in a later essay on narrative in the sensational stories of French tabloids: surely *those* fit into his interpretation even less.[61]

In the Tacitus text we have no paradigm of *innocent tools,* or rather of words denoting *tools* and connoting *innocence.* What we do have is a long, cumulative sequence of violent deaths, characterized, on the one hand, by a variety of lethal instruments that run the gamut from the most sophisticated weapons to any implement that chance may place at the executioner's disposal. On the other hand, there is the constant will to destroy. We are dealing here with a sequence of metaphors of the pertinacity of evil. The variousness of the tools, all used for the same purpose, lays stress—like a variety of figures with the same meaning (*similitude in dissimilitudine*)—upon the implacability of political death in imperial Rome. The most sophisticated weapons (the tricky ceiling, for instance) and the simplest tools (improvised on the spot by the journeymen of Death) are thus different only in appearance, for functionally they are synonymous. First, both sophistication and crudeness are polar extremes: their simultaneous effect is therefore the effect of a paradigm of hyperboles. Second, the polarity of efficient planning versus talented improvisation amounts to a statement of continuing, stubborn ingenuity in killers.

But where then did Barthes find *his* structure? It seems obvious to me that he found it not in Tacitus but in his own mind: all of us probably keep in mental storage somewhere the *criminal innocence* structure. In Barthes's case it irrupted from the reader's mind into his reading, thanks to the few textual data that fit. The contamination of the other data by this structure was made possible, if I may hazard a guess, by an obsession of his. Barthes several times in his writing comes back to what he feels is the *softness* of certain materials usually classified as hard. It will be recalled that he mentions this quality as a justification for referring to the innocence of tools. This obsessive motif, the paradoxical softness of hard materials, he alludes to in various texts; he goes so far as to coin words for it—always a significant clue for the structure-hunter (he speaks of *la tendreur du bois*). [62] And this motif is closely connected with one of the poles of our *criminal innocence* opposition: *softness* is indeed *innocence* translated into a wood-code or a stone-code or a hard-material-code.

Barthes, unlike the exegetes I discussed before, undoubtedly starts from data that are *stylistically marked* and *have* to be decoded. Yet we witness here a distortion of the actual structural model. I think this happens only because of the deceptive *latency* which the formalist definition of literary structures carries with it. That definition differentiates between the invariant model of relationships, which is the analyst's construct, and the variants which actualize it in the text. The critic translates this difference into affective meta-language, in the form of false but practical and tempting images: the *surface* and the *depth* of a text. It is then only too easy to hypothesize a contradiction between that surface and that depth (on the model of the archetypal opposition between appearance and reality).[63] In other words, the formalists on the one hand believe that every textual feature at the level of the signifiers (*signifiants*) is equally perceptible, but on the other hand they assume that the significata (*signifiés*) are not equally perceptible, being divided between a visible level and a hidden level. Barthes, I think, felt free to find a denominator common to a number of items that were not really relatable (or not relatable the way he suggests) because the ideas of *structure* and *latency* are usually associated. He felt free to make complete a similarity that was only partial (and therefore false) with the help of his own mythology, since the assumption of latency led him to transmute a nonexistence into a concealed existence. Of course *latency* is the wrong word: a structure (the invariant) is no more latent than geometry; it is simply an abstraction, like geometry. But its variants are quite tangible and are stylistically encoded.

I submit, then, that *the law of perceptibility extends to structures.* Not to the invariant, which is an abstract model, but to the variants. If we did not perceive them, we could not construct the model. And our decoding must be controlled, so as to make us perceive the textual segments that actualize the variants: perceive them not only as stylistically marked, but perceive them for what they are, in their function of variants, perceive them as correlates of something else.

Wherever a variant occurs, there are obviously features that make the reader feel a structural similarity exists between, say, the image in the text and other dissimilar images, which he suddenly connects with this one despite their unlikeness. In other words, if there is latency, it is a latency so encoded as 1) to reveal that there is something to be uncovered, and 2) to indicate how the uncovering is to be done. Style analysis should therefore precede any attempt to build the structural model of a text.

The French formalists have acted as idea-brokers; they

Michael Riffaterre

have exposed the ideologies underlying and distorting traditional French criticism. Above all, they have laid emphasis upon the verbal essence of literature and, it is to be hoped, have freed French textual analysis of its tendency towards sterile literality. But paradoxically it is in their very effort to combat such literality that their chief weakness manifests itself. As they search for the ideologies that are encoded in a text, for the plurality of its meanings, and for its structures, they pay too little heed to what it is in the text that insures a proper decoding: namely, its style.

COLUMBIA UNIVERSITY

NOTES

1. A thorough discussion of French formalism is obviously beyond the scope of this paper. I have limited myself to indicating where the French formalists' practice is not entirely consistent with either their theory or its implications; and to pointing out the need for corroboration of the structuralist approach by style analysis. The best general introductions to French new criticism are Serge Doubrovsky's *Pourquoi la nouvelle critique. Critique et objectivité* (Paris: Mercure de France, 1968), and Gérard Genette's *Figures,* vol. I (Paris: Ed. du Seuil, 1966), especially 145-170, 185-204, and 253-265. See also G. Poulet, ed., *Les Chemins actuels de la critique* (Paris: Union générale d'éditions, 1968). Most other writings on the subject unfortunately emanate from the University Establishment and they make hardly any effort to understand what Barthes and his group are trying to do. Doubrovsky rightly condemns "l'absence de tout systéme de pensée" in these attacks (*loc. cit.,* p. 11). The same applies to Robert E. Jones's *Panorama de la nouvelle critique en France* (Paris: SEDES, 1968), except that Jones is not aggressive. Despite his title, he ignores the French formalists as a group, deals very superficially with Barthes, and evidences no understanding of the idea of structure.

2. Not only do they have their own periodical, like many groups before them in French literary history (like the *NRF* people, or the Existentialist brigade attached to *Les Temps modernes*); they also

control a publishing house (Editions du Seuil), have a Center for weekly theoretical discussions (opened in May 1968), and exercise influence on *Critique,* another journal of ideas.

3. As early as 1963, Barthes himself conceded that the term would not be an oversimplification (essay in *Essais critiques,* Paris: Seuil, 1964, p. 253).

4. René Wellek, *Concepts of Criticism* (Yale Univ. Press, 1963), p. 279.

5. On the trends in style analysis, see Gerald Antoine "Le Stylisticien face a l'ancienne et a la nouvelle critique" in G. Poulet, ed., *Les Chemins actuels de la critique,* pp. 159-174; the September 1969 issue of *Langue française;* also Karl D. Uitti, *Linguistics and Literary Theory* (Englewood Cliffs: Prentice-Hall, 1969), and Bernard Dupriez, *L'Etude des styles* (Paris: Didier, 1969).

6. Barthes, *Essais critiques,* pp. 250-1. This does not mean that the work of art cannot be related to social conditions, psychological conditions, etc; only the analysis of inside data must precede any attempt to put the text back into its anthropological setting.

7. Paris: Seuil, 1965 (translations from Jakobson, Ejkhenbaum, Shklovskij, Vinogradox, Tynjanov, Brik, Tomashevskij, and Propp).

8. *Essais de linguistique generale* (Paris: Ed. de Minuit, 1963).

9. "*Les Chats* de Baudelaire" *L'Homme,* 2 (1962), 5-21. I have raised various objections to their approach in my "Describing Poetic Structures: Two Approaches to Baudelaire's *Les Chats*" in *Yale French Studies,* 36/37 (1966), 200-242. See also P. Delbouille, "Analyse structurale et analyse textuelle," *Cahiers d'Analyse textuelle* (Liège, Belgium), 10 (1968), 7-22; G. Mounin, "Baudelaire devant une critique structurale," *Annales de la Fac. des Lettres . . . de Nice,* 4-5 (1968), 155-160; and Wm. O. Hendricks, "Three Models for the Description of Poetry," *Journal of Linguistics,* 5 (1969), 1-22.

10. Also an entirely new essay, on another poem of Baudelaire's: "Une Microscopie du dernier Spleen dans les *Fleurs du Mal,*" *Tel Quel,* 29 (1967), 12-24.

11. On his six-function model of language communication, developed out of K. Bühler's three functions and J. Mukarovsky's esthetic function, see my remarks in *Proceeding of the Ninth International Congress of Linguists* (The Hague: Mouton, 1964), pp. 316-323.

12. Whose main contribution is *Sémantique structurale* (Paris: Larousse, 1966).

13. An important by-product of their activities is the scholarly magazine *Communications,* published by the *Centre d'études des communications de masse,* founded in 1960 at the Ecole by Georges Friedmann. No. 8 (1966), for instance, is devoted to the structural analysis of the narrative.

14. See her "Bakhtine, le mot, le dialogue et le roman," *Critique* 239 (1967), 438-465. Also *Tel Quel,* 35 (Fall 1968) on Russian "sémiologie."

15. E.g. Claude Bremond (whose starting point was Propp) "Le Message narratif," *Communications,* 4 (1964), 4-32, and "La Logique des possibles narratifs," *Communications,* 8 (1966), 60-76.

16. Wellek, *Concepts of Criticism,* pp. 57-58, 356-357.

17. Genette, *Figures,* I, 253-265.

18. Another introductor to linguistics is Emile Benveniste, especially his collection of papers *Problémes de linguistique générale,* (Paris: *NRF,* 1966). A splinter group gathered around J.-P. Faye is now trying one-upmanship on the *Tel Quel*ists by invoking Chomsky.

19. The controversy broke out when Barthes's *Sur Racine* (Paris: Ed. du Seuil, 1963) was subjected to a violent attack by a Sorbonne professor, Raymond Picard, in his *Nouvelle critique ou nouvelle imposture* (Paris: J. J. Pauvert, 1965). Barthes answered brilliantly with *Critique et Vérité* (Paris: Ed. du Seuil, 1966). Many others joined in the battle, including the mass media.

20. Barthes, *Essais critiques,* pp. 250-1.

21. Genette, *Figures,* I, 157; he quotes R. Jakobson, *Essais de ling. générale,* p. 74: "la linguistique structurale comme la mécanique quantique gagnent en determinisme morphique ce qu'elles perdent en déterminisme temporel."

22. Barthes justly argues that from a rational standpoint the complementarity of the different approaches should have invited peaceful coexistence (*Essais critiques,* p. 247). Cf. Doubrovsky, *Pourquoi,* pp. 87, 89-90. The political or even seemingly religious overtones in the indictment of formalism are well exemplified in Barthes's *Critique et vérité,, passim.*

23. On the concept of literariness (Russian *literaturnost*), see V. Erlich, *Russian Formalism* (The Hague: Mouton, 1955), pp. 146 ff. Also Todorov, ed., *Théorie de la littérature,* p. 37.

24. Barthes, *Critique et vérité,* p. 37.

25. French Classicism, as defined by French literary historians, is as

much a set of nationalistic clichés as it is a critical or historical entity (see L. F. Benedetto, "Le leggenda del classicismo francese," *Rassegna d'Italia,* 2 [1947], 3-21); illustrative of this attitude is Alexis François's *Histoire de la langue française cultivée* (Geneva: Jullien, 1959). On *clarté française,* see Barthes, *Critique et vérité,* pp. 27 ff.; Cf. Daniel Mornet, *Histoire de la clarté française* (Paris: Payot 1929).

26. See "La Révolution ici maintenant," *Tel Quel,* 34 (Summer 1968), 3-4. *Théorie d'ensemble* (Paris: Seuil, 1968) is a collection of reprints and a statement of the group's latest opinions. Of the contributors, Michel Foucault and Jacques Derrida are critics very much on their own; their work calls for a separate study. The novelist J. P. Faye is missing; he now leads a secessionist wing that publishes the journal *Changes.* A 1965 essay of R. Barthes is reprinted with a running commentary that traces the author's evolution since the first version. Two fundamental positions of the group transpire: first, they place critical thought in time, thereby consciously linking it with the attitudes, stereotypes, myths, and issues of that particular period and seeking to avoid all danger of unconscious contamination or rationalization of critical judgment by these factors. Second, they treat criticism itself as a text, hence an object of criticism. Not only do the critics interpret literature and society in the light of ideologies, but their interpretation is in turn to function as a factor in the further evolution of society and literature. (See especially, in *Théorie,* Sollers, pp. 318-25 and 399-405.

27. Erlich, *Russian Formalism,* pp. 96 ff., 134.

28. Valéry, Pléiade ed., vol. I, p. 1463 (my translation).

29. Sollers, *Logiques* (Paris: Seuil, 1968), pp. 198-205.

30. For instance, the development of Barthes's theory of literature was for a time closely connected with the Nouveau Roman and, more especially, with Robbe-Grillet. Jean Thibaudeau's critical thought "needed" Ponge's poetry. Sollers' concept of the novel presupposes the jeopardy or destruction of the genre's traditional features (e.g., Sollers, *Logiques,* pp. 226-49). Kristeva acknowledges that her definition of poetic language "works" better with texts from before or after the "bourgeois esthetics of Renaissance" ("Poésie et négativité," *L'Homme,* 8 [1968], p. 44), etc.

31. See Krystyna Pomorska, *Russian Formalist Theory and Its Poetic Ambiance* (The Hague: Mouton 1968).

32. Of Racine's plays Barthes writes: "Nous ne savons pas bien ce

qui est répresenté ici. Est-ce, selon l'hypothese de Darwin, un très vieux fonds folklorique, un état à peu près a-social de l'humanité? Est-ce, selon l'hypothèse de Freud, la toute première histoire de la psyché, reproduite dans l'enfance de chacun de nous? Je constate seulement que le théâtre racinien ne trouve sa cohérence qu'au niveau de cette fable ancienne, située très en arriere de l'histoire ou de la psyché humaine" (*Sur Racine,* p. 21). Needless to say, such a model is not an attempt at a psychoanalysis of the author. It is designed to translate literary discourse into psychoanalytical discoure, that is, to explain the characters and their relationships as variants of a psychological structure: "cette action originelle n'est pas jouée par des personnages, au sens moderne du mot: ... il s'agit au fond de masques, de figures qui reçoivent leurs différences, non de leur état civil, mais de leur place dans la configuration générale qui les tient enfermés. ... C'est la fonction qui les distingue. ... Aussi le discours racinien de grandes masses de langage indivis, comme si, à travers des paroles différentes, une seule et même personne s'exprimait" (*ibid*).

33. Barthes, *Critique et Vérité,* pp. 39-40.

34. Kristeva, for instance, defines the links between a text and an ideology or mythology (*mythologèmes*) as *intertextuality* ("interaction textuelle qui se produit *à l'intérieur d'un texte*" [my italics] between several codes—e.g., scholastic tradition, *poésie courtoise,* etc. in the text of a fifteenth-century novel) in *Théorie d'ensemble,* pp. 312-3; Cf. J. L. Baudry, *ibid.,* p. 54; J. L. Houdebine, pp. 296-7; Kristeva again, "Poésie et négativité," *L'Homme,* 8, p. 43. There is thus in literary text a superimposition of several discourses. (This model is an extrapolation of the concept of *paragramme* borrowed from Saussure by Starobinski and first used to describe parodic statements in Lautréamont: Cf. Kristeva, "Poésie et négativité.") Unfortunately, to describe intertextuality the formalists resort to a dichotomy between the "surface" and the "depths" of a text. Furthermore, they take for granted that the more or less complete deciphering depends upon the reader's culture (e.g., Sollers, *Logiques,* pp. 199-200). It seems to me, however, that a text is always "effective" independently of the reader's moods or aesthetic preferences. Which can be explained only if "intertextuality" is encoded in such a way as to make complete decoding imperative for all readers: it must therefore be observable at the signifiers' level, in the words themselves and in their groupings.

35. Ricardou, "L'Or du scarabee," *Theorie d'ensemble,* p. 377.

36. Ricardou is wrong because it is the English original version that he is interpreting, and because he lets himself be influenced by the French of Baudelaire's translation. Baudelaire had to avoid the French *huguenot* as a translation of the English *Huguenot* because in French mythology the word is inseparable from its associations with sixteenth-century religious wars, and it would therefore be archaic in a contemporary American context. By choosing the French word *protestant* instead, he hits upon what in French mythology corresponds to the type of the enterprising, self-reliant, sober Yankee Quaker in American mythology (whereas the English *Protestant* would have been downright tautology for Poe).

37. One French novel at least is built entirely upon this structural opposition and its transformation: Theophile Gautier's *Capitaine Fracasse* (1863).

38. Cf. Genette, in Poulet, ed., *Chemins actuels,* pp. 131-2, 136; *Figures,* I, pp. 259 ff.

39. Genette, *Figures,* I, p. 158; Cf. René Girard, "La Notion de structure en critique littéraire," Supplement to *Studi francesi,* 34 (January-April 1968), 64 ff., who prefers the term *critique-sujet.*

40. Girard, *loc. cit.,* p. 65 (the critic must "s'abandonner à l'objet").

41. Barthes, *Essais critiques,* p. 272.

42. Barthes, *Essais critiques,* pp. 255 ff.; Kristeva, "La Semiologie" in *Théorie d'ensemble,* p. 81. The elaboration of the metalanguage must take into account the *intertextuality* of the text (see fn. 34): Kristeva, in *Théorie d'ensemble,* p. 312 (see discussion by J. Peytard in *Linguistique et littérature,* special issue of *La Nouvelle Critique* (1968), p. 72; Cf. also Kristeva, "Pour une semiologie des paragrammes," *Tel Quel,* 29 (1967), 53-75.

43. The rule of isomorphism strikes down the objections of traditional criticism: when Picard charges formalists with choosing their metalanguage to please themselves, he simply fails to understand the difference between code and structure (Cf. Doubrovsky, *Pourquoi . . .* p. 83).

44. Barthes, *Critique et vérité,* p. 64.

45. *Ibid.,* pp. 65-66.

46. Barthes, *Essais critiques,* pp. 270-1.

47. Barthes, *Critique et vérité,* p. 20.

48. *Ibid.*, p. 41.

49. Cf. Erlich, *Russian Formalism*, p. 158.

50. *Ibid.*, pp. 150-1.

51. *Théorie d'ensemble,* p. 379. I pass over other interpretations, such as *William* (name of the man who deciphers Captain Kidd's will) as the anagram of *I am (the) will* (p. 378), etc.

52. The examples just given may seem so ridiculous that I may be suspected of having picked on a weak opponent, some unimportant epigone of the Movement. Ricardou is not that: he is an esteemed practitioner of the new *nouveau roman,* the type approved by the *Tel Quel* team and printed in their press. He is the theoretician of this new novel in his useful *Problèmes du nouveau roman* (1967). Further, the theologians of the Movement obviously find his conclusions exemplary: not only was the paper I have been discussing published in *Tel Quel,* 34 (Summer 1968), it was chosen for inclusion in *Théorie d'ensemble* as one of the still-rare practical applications of the theory. So we must regard this paper as representative.

53. E.g., Barthes, *Critique et vérité,* p. 65.

54. Cf. fn. 11.

55. Sollers, *Logiques,* p. 90; Pleynet, *Théorie d'ensemble,* p. 342, fn. 9.

56. Sade, *Opuscules sur le Theatre,* quoted by Pleynet himself.

57. Unless we interpret *-wil* as the anglicization (and therefore the hyperbolization) of an aristocratic *Clairville.* Further proof that the name even in its French spelling is already noble enough, lies in the fact that it was chosen as a pen name by the vaudevillist Nicolaie (1811-1879). That *-wil* is a purely exotic suffix is demonstrated by names such as *mylord Barwil* in Sade's "Miss Henriette Stralson" (*Les Crimes de l'Amour,* Pauvert ed., II, p. 222).

58. In Todorov ed., *Théorie de la littérature,* p. 294. The rule *I* should think applies here (and probably to most eighteenth-century French novels as well) is that the only names with a meaning are those of secondary characters and of supernumeraries, while the protagonists' names simply carry social status markers. Secondary characters need be distinguished only by their trades or habits, and they are likely to be reified. It is significant that they are often comical or caricatural, which goes hand in hand with reification (or any simplification). A parallel can be drawn with the masters' habit of substituting "descriptive"

names for their servants' patronymics (or first names). E.g., in Sade's text a "maffioso" is called *Brisa-Testa* ("Head-Breaker") and a banker— much despised at the time—is called *Mondor* ("Mountain of Gold"). I find the same name and the same character ridiculed in Abbé Delille's versified *Epître sur le luxe* (1774). The protagonists' names admit of no such reading: it is enough that they are described as members of an elite. In terms of the novel, this indicates that they are people of means and leisure and are thus in a position to put their own philosophy into practice, that they stand above social laws and are free of economic pressures.

59. "Tacite et le baroque funèbre," *Essais critiques,* p. 110.

60. E.g., Pierre Albouy, *La Création mythologique chez V. Hugo,* pp. 161-4. Comparable themes can be found in Cocteau (e.g., *Portraits-Souvenir,* 1935, p. 152).

61. *Essais critiques,* p. 193.

62. Barthes, *Mythologies* (Paris: Seuil 1957), p. 64; Cf. *Essais critiques,* p. 21. *Tendreur* is a portmanteau word built on *tendresse,* used only of human beings, and *douceur; tendreté,* used for meat, for example, is clearly avoided because it would not evoke feeling, especially intimate feeling.

63. This procedure is made even more tempting by the psychoanalytic approach. But it is in fact a kind of intentional fallacy. If my understanding of latency is correct, Genette's partial reservations concerning structural analysis as practiced by the formalists will no longer be necessary (see *Figures,* I, pp. 158-9).

MYTH AND IDENTITY CRISIS IN
A MIDSUMMER NIGHT'S DREAM

René Girard

It can be shown, I believe, that Greek mythology, notably the Oedipus myth, is born of a crisis so radical in its scope, so far-reaching in its implications that no standard approach, be it religious, historical, sociological, psychoanalytical, will do justice to it. Only ambiguous traces of this crisis remain; among them the many conflicts of *enemy brothers,* or even *enemy twins,* the irreconcilable struggle of those separated by no difference whatever.[1]

"Values" will clash because they are different and cannot be reconciled. The idea of a conflict rooted not in differences but in their absence, of a conflict irreconcilable because there is nothing to reconcile, is repugnant to Western thought. This repugnance is even written into the language. Of people who cannot live in harmony, we say that "they have their differences," not that they have lost them. Un "differénd" in French, means quarrel, dispute, conflict.

Myth itself is far from equivocal on the subject. Myth embodies both the disintegration and recomposition of differences. It may be defined as the account of its own genesis, retrospectively transfigured by the re-establishment of differences. If culture is defined as an ordered system of differences, the crisis from which mythical literature originates is a crisis of culture as a whole and of all its parts, a collapse of all cultural differences.

Myth proper is the crisis of differences only mythically remembered. The countless manners in which differences are transgressed, disregarded, obliterated, make up the variety of myth. Thus, transgression of differences, parricide, incest, bestiality, hermaphroditism, etc. will be attributed to creatures who already partake of several modes of being, sharply differentiated in normal times, semi-gods, monsters that are half man and half beast, etc.

Greek tragedy and the tragic mode generally flourish in periods of religious and cultural crisis. Tragedy plunges myth back into its original atmosphere, in the acid milieu where differences and old myths are corroded and decomposed, only to be revivified. Turning away from the more fantastic aspects of myth, the tragic poet retrieves the irreconcilable conflict of the brothers which nourishes his art. In tragedy, some general assumptions concerning differences and their role in conflict are not valid or not always valid.

Shakespeare, in this respect, is a true heir to the Greeks. The famous speech of Ulysses, in *Troilus and Cressida,* is a case in point. The "degree" of Ulysses is equivalent, up to a point, to what I call "differences":

. . . Oh, when degree is shaked,
Which is the ladder to all high designs,
The enterprise is sick! How could communities,
Degrees in schools and brotherhoods in cities,
Peaceful commerce from dividable shores,
The primogenitive and due of birth,
Prerogative of age, crowns, scepters, laurels,
But by degree, stand in authentic place?

Take but degree away, untune that string,
And hark, what discord follows! Each thing meets
In mere oppugnancy. The bounded waters
Should lift their bosoms higher than the shores,
And make a sop of all this solid globe.
Strength should be lord of imbecility,
And the rude son should strike his father dead.
Force should be right, or rather, right and wrong,
Between whose endless jar justice resides,
Should lose their names, and so should justice too.
Then everything includes itself in power,
Power into will, will into appetite,
And appetite, a universal wolf,
So doubly seconded with will and power,
Must make perforce a universal prey,
And last eat up himself.

Degree is written in the singular, implying a perception of culture as an ordered system of degrees, or of differences, the definition given above. Degree is the unifying principle of a totality. Such perception of culture prevails, quite often, in times of crisis, when culture as a whole is threatened. The apocalyptic nature of the passage just quoted is an eloquent witness to the presence of that threat.

Degree as a unifying and sacred principle as well as a system of differences, degree as *hierarchy* in both the etymological and modern acceptations of the term, is made more vivid still by the metaphor of the musical string: *Untune that string and hark what discord follows!* Discord, thus, is the fruit not of differences but of their loss; discord opposes beings undifferentiated or not differentiated enough, unspecified and ill-defined "things," not even capable of meaningful disagreement. *Each thing meets in mere oppugnancy.* Unable to find the way, men err, deprived of their "identity" and individuality; they collide endlessly and stupidly as they are tossed by the storm, like physical objects, when they lose their moorings on the deck of a ship. Community and brotherhood are gone. Jacob and Esau are back. So is Oedipus: . . . *And the rude son should strike his father dead.*

*   *   *

In many parts of the world, along with myths, certain customs appear to commemorate, even re-enact the "shaking of degree." Folk festivals vary in detail but some essential features are common to a number of them. During the festival, hierarchies and social differences are disregarded. Servants do not serve their masters; children do not obey their parents, wives their husbands, inferiors their superiors. Sexual promiscuity may be tolerated, even encouraged. Disguises and transvestitism are common.

Transgression is too negative a word to encompass all aspects of these celebrations which are not focused, really, on the crisis but on the recovery of differences. The Bachanalia in Greece and, in Rome, the Saturnalia belong to the category just defined. In England, seasonal celebrations, such as May Day and Midsummer Night, were still very much alive in the days of Shakespeare, even though frowned upon by the Protestant church. The crisis of Difference is the main common ground, I believe, between the midsummer festival and *A Midsummer Night's Dream,* a ground very consciously and strategically occupied by the author.

Nature itself is involved in that crisis. We are told that the weather was bad when the play was written. No doubt, but even extraordinarily bad weather would not be brought up there if there were not some extra-meteorological reason for doing so, if the weather were not to be discussed in a special, peculiarly Shakespearian manner. In Ulysses' speech, natural as well as cultural disorders, in a passage just before the one quoted above, are attributed to a loss of degree, to the plants wandering in "evil mixture," to their straying from properly differentiated orbits. In *A Midsummer Night's Dream,* bad weather is the blotting out of seasonal differences. In the eyes of Titania, recent floods and other vagaries of nature are a destruction of Difference and that destruction is caused by her own conflict with the being she is normally closest to, her king Oberon:

> . . . The spring, the summer,
> The childing autumn, angry winter, change
> Their wonted liveries, and the mazed world,
> By their increase, now knows not which is which.
> And this same progeny of evils comes
> From our debate, from our dissension.
> We are their parents and original.

We may note that Shakespeare reverses, here, the relationship between nature and myth long taken for granted by the modern world. He may well suggest, by the way, the more fecund direction for the understanding of myth. Myth is not an "imperfect science" because it is not intended as an explanation of nature. Modern man believes, in his self-centered pride, that myth tries to achieve, and fails, what he himself tries to achieve, and succeeds, namely an understanding of nature *per se,* nature isolated from man. This is never the case. Natural phenomena are brought into myth as a metaphor of what happens to man, as one more element in a global interpretation of reality entirely dominated by the fate of the community, i.e. by the historical vicissitudes of Difference. Men can be relatively at peace with each other and with themselves in a relatively benevolent nature, and they can be beset by strife, and nature itself partakes in the rampage. Nature, then, becomes "evil mixture," a warring confusion of all that should be kept separate, a dissolution and liquefaction of all that was formerly solid and well defined. The Flood is a logical and fundamental expression of a cultural apocalypse defined as loss of Difference. As Ulysses says:

> . . . The bounded waters
> Should lift their bosoms higher than the shores
> And make a sop of all this solid globe.

The conflict of Titania and Oberon parallels, on the "supernatural" plane, the conflict of the four lovers which is the main "action," in *A Midsummer Night's Dream,* and which deserves most attention. In his truly admirable and indispensable study of *Shakespeare's Festive Comedies,* C. L. Barber has shown that the folk festivals provide the playwright with more than a pretext or convenient setting. The critic also notes, in *A Midsummer Night's Dream,* the progressive disappearance of differences between the four lovers. Unlike many interpreters, he does not view this disappearance as something purely negative, as a dramatic imperfection rather difficult to explain with a creator of such stature. It is not uncommon to read about the "insufficient characterization" of the four lovers. Shakespeare's anti-psychologism is confused with bad psychology.

On midsummer night, the two couples run off into the woods, just as tradition demands, even though they do not have its observance in mind. There, relations of requited and unrequited love which appeared stable at the opening of the play are set in motion, so to speak, and, before the end of the night, all the various entanglements of jealousy, rivalry, fascination, and hatred, nearly all the unhappy combinations which the foursome can provide, will be exhausted. Barber observes that the four young people vainly try to interpret their conflicts through something "manageably related to their individual identities." These identities become more and more elusive as the game progresses. At one point, Helena finds that Hermia, her best friend and "sister," has joined hands with the two young men who have "turned against her." Helena feels that her friend is no longer true to her "real" personality and reproaches her for it:

Fie, fie! You counterfeit, you puppet you.

Hermia misunderstands these words and retorts:

Puppet? Why so? Ay, that way goes the game.
Now I perceive that she hath made compare
Between our statures; she hath urg'd her height.
. . .
How low am I? Thou painted maypole? Speak! —
How low am I?. . . .

Barber comments as follows:

. . . only accidental differences can be exhibited. Helena
tall, Hermia short. Although the men think that "reason
says" now Hermia, now Helena is "the worthier maid,"
personalities have nothing to do with the case. . . . The
life in the lovers' part is not to be caught in individual
speeches, but by regarding the whole movement of the
farce, which swings and spins each in turn through a
common pattern, an evolution that seems to have an
impersonal power of its own.

At the paroxysm of the night, the four lovers no longer
know, literally, who they are:

Am I not Hermia? Are not you Lysander?

Shakespeare, obviously, is trying to make a point and he will
never make it if we mistake it for "insufficient characterization." Characterization means differences. Character is not
"insufficient," therefore, through some fault or oversight of
the author, it is gradually effaced and erased as differences
themselves are effaced and erased. And all this, of course, is
intentional and premeditated.

The four lovers of comedy are really not different from

the *enemy brothers* of tragedy. There is nothing pleasant in the game they play. Shakespeare makes that point quite clear and he means every word of it even if the basic unpleasantness of it all is pleasantly stated, as demanded by the genre, as permitted, too, by the irresistible vocation of the characters themselves for self-induced misery, a trait beautifully evident in the following lines:

> Before the time I did Lysander see,
> Seemed Athens as a paradise to me.
> Oh then, what graces in my love do dwell,
> That he has turned a heaven unto a hell.

Love must be Hell in order to be worthy of the name. The *love* Hermia, and much of our literature, are talking about is a most unlikely label applied to an erotic variety of the tragic conflict, the conflict between the same and the same. This truth is not really hidden; it keeps asserting itself even in the tritest metaphors of passion which must be read, here, literally. When Shakespeare has Demetrius say:

> Where is Lysander and fair Hermia?
> The one I'll slay, the other slayeth me.

he is not guilty of "concessions to the taste of the time" any more than he was guilty of "insufficient characterization" before. The bad conceit is better here than a good one; it reinserts into its original context of brotherly, even physical conflict, the metaphor of passion, thus revealing still pleasantly no doubt, and ironically, but quite pointedly, its true filiation and veritable implications. The lovers know not what they say; we only have to listen, if we are in the slightest interested, and the truth will be ours.

What are the enemy brothers of Greek tragedy after? They are after their father's inheritance which keeps dwindling before their greedy eyes as they try to wrench it from each other. The prize disappears as it becomes an object of dispute because it is not physical but spiritual; it is *degree* itself, Difference which appears in various illusory forms to the warring brothers; it is the authority of the kind, the omni-science of the prophet, the prowess of the lover. As *hier-archy,* in the sense of an ordered system of differences, disintegrates, *hierarchy,* in the sense of sacred principle, be-comes an object of desire. Each brother tries to prevent the other from reaching hybristically for the sacred that must remain inviolate. Each brother thinks only the other one is guilty of hybris.

Thus, loss of differences goes hand in hand with the desire for it, each being apprehended now as the cause, now as the consequence of the other. This aspect is much in evidence as "pride," in *A Midsummer Night's Dream:* the lovers are overbearing, even insulting to each other. In nature too, "evil mixture," loss of differences is the consequence of a hybristic reaching for excessive Difference:

Contagious fogs, which falling on the land
Have every pelting river made so proud
That they have overborne their continents. . . .

What particular version of sacred Difference are the lovers fighting over? They dream of some absolute power of seduc-tion, of the self-sufficiency and near divine autonomy which is desired by all and which desires no one. This erotically mystical prize eludes each and everybody's grasp; thus, each of the four quickly finds himself in the unenviable position of believing that one of the remaining three has appropriated, "vizarded" as Ulysses would say, the invisible prize. Only negative clues can signal the presence of the hidden treasure; indifference, rejection, contempt. No one can win the game unless he appears as that "hard-hearted adamant" that draws all other, presumably softer, hearts to himself, without himself being drawn. Through the symmetry of language as well as of actions, Shakespeare underlines the systematic nature of what is unfolding, the reciprocity of non-reciprocal relationships:

> Hermia: The more I hate, the more he follows me.
> Helena: The more I love, the more he hateth me.

They all live in constant discord, not because anyone desires something different but because they all desire the same thing: Difference. Their actual impulses are so mimetic and undifferentiated that, at every given moment, they all run together to the same object, be it themselves or another, like children who all want to play with the same toy, only to give it up a second later, all together again. Thus, they can all believe they are most different when they are most alike.

Because the erotic absolute appears fleetingly incarnated by everyone in turn, the total configuration keeps changing in kaleidoscopic fashion, but nothing really changes except for the accelerating tempo of the vertiginous movement, obviously moving toward some sort of paroxystic resolution, the true nature of which will be eluded through the magic Puck.

*   *   *

Thus, Difference lost, desired, and ultimately recovered, provides the true common denominator, in *A Midsummer Night's Dream,* between the various themes which the estheticism, psychologism, and *Naturphilosophie* of recent criticism cannot reconcile and comprehend as a unit.

Another difference which is "wizarded" in the play is the difference between the supernatural and natural worlds. Haughty Titania finds, to her dismay, that the barrier is down between mortals and immortals:

Tell me how it came this night
That I sleeping there was found
With these mortals on the ground.

The grotesque love affair between the queen of the fairies
and a Bottom partly metamorphosed into an ass makes it
discreetly but unmistakably clear that the whole range of
mythical monstrosity is upon us. And this return of the
monstrous takes place in the most appropriate context of a
folk festival which re-enacts the crisis of the difference, in
other words the true process of myth creation.

Ostensibly, all is due to the magic of Puck and Oberon.
But magic, like the monstrous, is a product of myth making,
it cannot be its explanation. Magic is not Shakespeare's final
word any more than its rational and romantic counterparts,
"dream" and individual "imagination" however loudly and
frequently these may be invoked in the play itself and its
title. To maintain that *A Midsummer Night's Dream* is only a
potpourri of "magic," "dream," and "imagination," is to
equate it with any of a thousand mythological and fairyland
arrangements produced by the court cultures of Europe
between the Renaissance and the eighteenth century.

The tragic conflict of the brothers or, here, the misfor-
tunes of our four lovers are a more likely matrix of myth
creation than individual dreams and imagination. The scanda-
lous intermingling of god and beast in the episode of Bottom
and Titania has a metaphorical analogue in the language of a
"love" that humiliates and even degrades the lover to lower
and lower depths as it exalts the loved one to greater and
greater heights. Ultimately, such "love" is the experience of
nothingness in front of the All, of the lowly beast in front of
a god:

No, no, I am as ugly as a bear.
For beasts that meet me run away for fear.

> Therefore no marvel though Demetrius
> Do, as a monster, fly my presence thus.
> What wicked and dissembling glass of mine
> Made me compare with Hermia's sphery eyne?

The correspondence between the metaphoric and the thematic uses of beast and god is too obvious not to be intended. It must be understood within the framework of the play's openly acknowledged preoccupation with myth making. The language of this play, however, points to an answer more complex and more disturbing than Theseus's, even though it is still compatible with it:

> Such tricks has strong imagination
> That if it would but apprehend some joy,
> Or in the night, imagining some fear,
> How easy is a bush supposed a bear!

The god/beast polarity is really a consequence of the quest for Difference, or it translates, rather, the consequences of that quest into a certain metaphorical language. Helena would not see herself changed into a bear if she did not desire to be a god; it is the failure of that desire which turns the other into a god and the self into its opposite, a thing of contempt, a beast, a monster of ugliness. The two metamorphoses, the conjunction of god and beast in Titania and Bottom, as well as in the language of the four lovers are two correlative aspects of the same failure at erotic self-divinization. The study of myth, in the Greek world more particularly, would reveal that mythical creation also depends on a "partnership in fascination," of the kind microcosmically described by Shakespeare in the configuration of the four lovers.

The Pascalian *qui fait l'ange fait la bête* gives us the law of this particular mythical creation, provided, of course, it is made fully reciprocal. The other is always an angel when the self is a beast, a beast when the self is an angel. Bottom is not the only one, in other words, who makes an ass of himself. Difference now goes one way, now the other but it always appears to separate the lovers. They never really find out that they are all alike, that the other is an identical twin, separated by no difference, no distance whatever, a neighbor, *proximus.*

* * *

A Midsummer Night's Dream operates on two levels; on the "upper" level, the plot is the uncritical product of the mytho-poetic process: a reactionary father separates two touchingly loving young people. . . . Fairies intervene in human affairs. . . . An ass-headed Bottom makes love to a goddess. . . . On the "underground" level of language and desire, Shakespeare undermines his own mytho-poetic credibility, through the constant reference of metaphor to plot and plot to metaphor, through the counterpoint between the realistic interplay of rival desires and the pointedly fantastic and spurious *raison d'être* that is exhibited.

Many critics are understandably eager to remain on the upper level where romantic imagination and the good fairies reign supreme. Everything there is so much more gentlemanly and *literary,* so much less confusing and "dialectical." But it is becoming more and more difficult to ignore the "underground." The history of modern sensibility resembles a protracted and constantly aggravated repeat performance of our four lovers' identity crisis. We may be much closer to myth than we think but unable to reach any resolution; our endless midsummer night never leads to a cathartic liberation and fully crystallized mythical creation.

The perversions of desire with which our literature is

replete can easily be read into the various figures of the midsummer ballet. Sadism and masochism, for instance, cannot be viewed as separate elements which were not here before and which enter the picture at a definite moment. They may appear as such to the observer who becomes suddenly aware of their presence but they were implicit in all animal metaphors and, ultimately, in the definition of desire as the attempted "wizarding" of Difference:

> I am your spaniel, and, Demetrius,
> The more you beat me, I will fawn on you,
> Use me but as your spaniel, spurn me, strike me,
> Neglect me, lose me—only give me leave,
> Unworthy as I am, to follow you.
> What worser place can I beg in your love—
> And yet a place of high respect with me—
> Than to be used as your dog?

Such "masochism" cannot fail to be a part of the picture and the fact that animal metaphors may be borrowed from Ovid has nothing to do with that truth. The masochism of Hermia has no specific essence which could really distinguish her desire from that of the other three lovers, makes it more individual. The same can be said of the homosexual "overtones" in the attitude of Helena toward Hermia. Helena says she loves Demetrius but she appears even more fascinated by Hermia whom Demetrius loves than by Demetrius himself:

> Your eyes are lodestars, and your tongue's sweet air
> More tunable than lark to shepherd's ear
> When wheat is green, when hawthorn buds appear.
> Sickness is catching. Oh, were favor so,
> Yours would I catch, fair Hermia, ere I go.
> My ear should catch your voice, my eye your eye,
> My tongue should catch your tongue's sweet melody.
> Were the world mine, Demetrius being bated,
> The rest I'd give to be to you translated.

This *translation* from Helena's being into Hermia is a perfect definition of what the quest for Difference is about. Helena, here, rather than Demetrius, incarnates Difference because, as the successful rival, she appears more truly endowed with overpowering erotic superiority than the loved one himself. Thus, she becomes the invincible one, the "hard-hearted adamant." Desire orients itself toward the rival of the same sex.

This phenomenon illustrates perfectly the definition given above. Far from seeking sameness, close relatedness, as it may falsely claim, desire always seeks the maximum sexual difference. And this maximum difference is sought, ultimately, where none resides, namely in the same sex. Desire abolishes differences as it seeks them and it seeks them where there are none. It runs headlong into the non-difference which it perceives as extreme difference.

The question of homosexual "overtones" *in the text* is quite independent from its possible biographical implications. We may even say that, up to a point, it is independent from the author's intention and we do not mean by this statement that anything whatsoever is called into being by this author's "unconscious," we mean that the homosexual overtones are a necessary element in an intersubjective configuration generated by desire when it is defined as a quest for Difference; this element will appear whenever the consequences of the definition are systematically pursued. We said before that the quest for Difference tends to exhaust all possible pairings between the four lovers, without regard for sex differences, even as it retains its sexual definition. Homosexuality cannot fail to be included in that definition.

*   *   *

When the night is over, peace and harmony return. The folk festival is over. Thus, nature, the fairies, the whirl of conflicting desires, animal imagery, Bottom and Titania, all these thematic and linguistic elements contribute to the main thrust of the play; they embody various aspects of a "crisis of Difference" which never really turns out of control, exactly like the folk festival itself, the true nature of which is perfectly grasped. No stage more appropriate could be found for this ironic decomposition and recomposition of myth.

Difference is restored. Ulysses would say that "everything," once more, stands "in authentic place." How is this miracle achieved, when no Puck is available? How is it achieved outside of the theater, outside of the folk festival, when the crisis is real? Going back for a moment to ethnological considerations, we will turn our attention toward the curious fashion in which, as a general rule, the seasonal festivals are terminated. A variety of demons and spirits, generally "evil," sometimes the devil himself, are violently expelled from the community in a solemn ceremony. This explusion is often accomplished by a wild beating of the air, accompanied by a terrifying din, all of this being perhaps less self-interpreting than it appears.

The real import of these actions may be guessed from those rituals where the expulsion proper is preceded by a heated debate between the participants, a simulated quarrel, even exchanges of blows. Violence against the devil alone may be a typically mythical adulteration of what is still remembered more correctly as *reciprocal* violence in some rituals. This reciprocal violence must be carefully distinguished from the expulsion that follows. The expulsion proper must be interpreted as the re-enactment of a violence which did, really, put an end to the crisis because it was unanimous and unilateral rather than reciprocal and divisive like all previous violence.

An analysis of Oedipus reveals that the perfect symmetry of all rapports within the thematic structure of the myth is destroyed by the expulsion of the hero.[2] Unless we question the entire content of the myth, the expulsion will never be perceived as arbitrary *because it determines the very nature of that content.* There is no *difference,* really, between the criminal "parricide" and "incest" of the scapegoat on the one hand, and that contagious plague which hits a passive and innocent city on the other. Only arbitrary violence can *make the Difference.* Only arbitrary violence can generate the "crimes" of the scapegoat and the "illness" of the city, the two contrasting metaphors which substantiate that difference and which remove from our view the one and only reality behind both, which is, of course, the crisis of Difference, the more and more reciprocal, and less and less differentiated conflict which threatens the whole community.

Thus is vertiginous reciprocity eliminated and the "contagion" of "evil mixture" warded off. The violent differentiation between the scapegoat and his executors is the original Difference, which brings all others back.

How is this phenomenon possible? How can divisive, reciprocal violence become unanimous, unilateral, and re-unifying? As the conflict of the "enemy brothers" exasperates, as the oscillation of Difference accelerates, reciprocity becomes more perfect and each individual becomes the other's mirror image, his *double.* This *double* is the same as the *Doppelgänger* of German romanticism but it must not be a pretext for confusing vagueness and the fantastic developments to which it is, paradoxically but demonstrably, alien. The *double* is the "enemy twin" in its extreme form, the fascinating rival who is both an object of "love" and hatred; he is Hermia to Helena and Helena to Hermia; he is Lysander to Demetrius and Demetrius to Lysander; he is that obsessive *other* who appears as extreme Difference because he is absolutely the same, the other who cannot fail to cross the subject's path at every turn since he seems to duplicate in reverse—inside the mirror—everything that subject does, thinks, desires, *is.*

Far from being a "dream," poetic fancy, or the product of

"imagination" as Theseus, the romantic poets and Dr. Jacques Lacan will maintain, this *double* is the closest approximation of reality ever perceived from inside the system. The *double* is the end product of the quest for Difference as it became mediated by others and turns into that mimetic desire which cannot fail to multiply its own obstacles, only to be further exasperated by them.

In myth and in Greek tragedy, as well as in romantic, once more and in modern literature, enigmatic references to the *double* are common and they come, as a rule, just before or after the violent resolution of the crisis. In the course of the night, as the lovers gradually lose, or should we say, as they find their true *identities*—the *identity crisis,* too, is written into the language since the word identity means both itself and its opposite; we may choose which is which (and one might wish, by the way, that our psychiatrists give a thought or two to that curious duality before they presume to solve our identity crisis)—they turn into the *doubles* of one another; it is no surprise, therefore, but it is nevertheless striking to find an overt, if ironical, reference to the *double* when the characters wake up, the morning after:

Hermia: Methinks I see these things with parted eye,
       When everything seems double.
Helena: So methinks.

Why is the *double* associated to both the paroxysm and the resolution of the conflict? When everyone is the *double* of everyone else, conditions are realized for a sacrificial substitution, for a single individual to take the place of all others as the universal butt of all fascination and hatred. When "the universal wolf," to use Ulysses' words, has made "perforce" a "universal prey," any single wolf can pounce on any single prey; all the wolves, therefore, may suddenly decide to pounce on the same prey. Their unanimity will hide the arbitrary nature of that violent act. The isolated prey will really appear as the bearer of all impure and malevolent forces which beset the community. Because its unanimous destruction will really break the vicious circle of morbid desire, the rival appropriation and preservation of Difference.

The scapegoat partakes of two worlds; the embodiment of all the ills that plague the city, he becomes, through his expulsion, the cure. He is doubly fated, therefore, to inherit all the obsessive polarities which plague the *doubles* and to become the devilish-holy monster, the sacred receptacle of all "evil mixture." Tragic and mythical heroes, semi-gods, full-blown divinities are only stages in the sacralization of the whole scapegoat process.

The expulsion differentiates once more the profane and the sacred, the original difference from which all others proceed. Not only is the scapegoat the agent through which Difference is restored, he is also the indispensable basis for all fully developed mythical creation. He, alone, can provide a stabler anchor point, and insure the crystallization of the angel/beast dichotomy described above as well as of other possible mythical polarities. Thus, the mythology of a highly differentiated cultural system can be entirely dedicated to the formerly evil, and now holy, undifferentiation brought about by Difference itself, when it was disputed between the enemy twins.

The object of the folk festival is not a repetition but a prevention of the crisis. "Evil mixture" is never re-enacted for its own sake, as our insufficiently emancipated puritans always believe, "evil mixture" is only a prologue to the main event, which is the expulsion of the "spirits." The folk festival attempts to revive or to perpetuate the curative power of a collective violence which is never perceived as such. Collective violence is both the source and the first object of mythical transfiguration. The expulsion may be not only metamorphosed but completely omitted from the final construct. The expulsion expels itself, so to speak but its effects remain, not only in myth and in the folk festival but in the theater and, perhaps, throughout Western cultural and intellectual life.

*　　*　　*

We have no scapegoat, no expulsion to mar the joy of happy resolution, in *A Midsummer Night's Dream;* not a drop of blood is shed; yet, the effects of the expulsion are all there. Reconciled Oberon and Titania leave humans alone and rejoin their separate domain. Lysander will marry Hermia and Demetrius Helena. With the sacred and the profane separate once more, everything "stands in its authentic place."

If the resolution of the play is one with the resolution of the folk festival, it stems from the same source, arbitrary violence, whether we have a victim or not. We may well question, therefore, the "authenticity" of everyone's "place." Even if the final arrangement spells they-were-married-and-lived-happily-forever-after, we cannot really believe that it was preordained by the good fairies or decreed by eternal nature in its infallible wisdom. With the sacred and the profane neatly differentiated once more, so are individuals, ideas, sentiments, and concepts, or at least so do they appear. That is why the critics who deal with *A Midsummer Night's Dream* at the level of "magic," "dream," and "fantasy" are also the ones who believe in the "psychology"—insufficient, of course—of the four lovers, and in the purely *aesthetic* nature—whatever that means—of the whole enterprise.

"Love" is no longer dangerously akin to "hate," "pride" is no longer the queer bedfellow of "humiliation." Promiscuousness between the "beasts" and the "gods" is no longer tolerated. The beasts are returned to Ovid and the fairies to

English folklore, where they belong. The unity of *A Mid-summer Night's Dream* is purely formal, or perhaps circumstantial.

Critics, too, need their cathartic resolutions. But is their conceptual order a true reflection of platonic essences in their unchanging realm, or is it only the merry-go-round of the four lovers that has ceased to spin for a while? When degree is being "shaked," individual "places," ideas, concepts, and sentiments are being constantly exchanged and this wild exchange is no more and no less *authentic* than the former stability. Even at its most permanent and respectable, degree is rooted in a violence which may not always kill a scapegoat but always destroys the symmetry, identity, and reciprocity which is the truth of the tragic brothers.

Degree as hidden violence is certainly more livable and tolerable than degree as open violence but the two are not really very *different* from each other. The "shaking" of degree is really the emergence of degree's original and primordial violence into the light of day. Degree, ultimately, *is not;* it does not exist as an object of worship, when it spells "law and order," any more than as an object of desire, when it spells disorder and violence. Degree is myth *par excellence.* Men get a little close to the truth only when degree is being "shaked" so much, that it becomes blurred in the loss of all identities, only when the obsessive *double* begins to haunt their perception.

The double is the truth of the configuration of desire, non-difference piercing through the illusion of extreme Difference, the *proximity* of the brother, the sameness of the neighbor trying vainly to assert itself beneath the mad oscillations of the angels and the beasts. But no real knowledge is ever reached through violence. The presence of the *double*, in literature, always ushers in sheer lunacy or that cathartic violence which will stabilize Difference once more.

The repression of the truth always coincides with its emergence since the paroxysm of the conflict brings both the *double* and the one-sided resolution. In *A Midsummer Night's Dream,* for instance, the all-important *double* is only a brief allusion, strategically located at the very moment when "these things," already less visible, are beginning to recede into the distance:

> like far off mountains turned into clouds

Good Theseus is back to make "these things" look more reassuring still with his famous refrain:

> The lunatic, the lovers, the poet
> Are of imagination all compact.

Hippolita tugs Theseus at the sleeve to warn him that his neat differentiation between the "imaginary" and the "real," like all neat differentiations, may leave something to be desired:

> But all the story of the night told over,
> And all their mindes transfigured so together,
> More witnesseth than fancy's images.
> And grows to something of great constancy,
> But, howsoever, strange and admirable.

Theseus hears nothing. He is too much like Ulysses, and so are we, not to remain at least partially deaf. Hippolita has been tugging at that sleeve for close to four hundred years, now, with no consequence whatever, a victim of catharsis too, eternally silenced by that same pressing need to blunt the sharp edge of Shakespeare's genius which produces such gems as "insufficient characterization."

But that genius will give us no rest. Hippolita's subversive lines are not its last word in *A Midsummer Night's Dream.* The ironically anticathartic mood will assert itself once more in *Pyramus and Thisbe.*

Is it really a wall that stands between young Pyramus and beautiful Thisbe? Obviously not since the two can meet where and when they wish, without any hindrance. When the wall has walked out, the lion marches in, but the undoing of the lovers has nothing to do with either of these carefully timed untimely obstacles. The lion is as innocent of killing them as the wall is ineffectual in keeping them apart.

That wall and that lion that come and go like real people are only mythical obstacles of the kind Shakespeare himself must also resort to, out of respect for the conventions of his genre and the demands of the audience—the fairies, for instance, and also the reactionary father, Egeus, who must be trotted in and out at the beginning and the end of the play in order to satisfy the spectator's expectations.

Early in the play, Lysander and Hermia enumerate, in true romantic fashion, the obstacles in the path of "true love." Solid obstacles, as hard as walls, hostile and irreducible differences brought to bear from outside on a passion no less unique, original, unshakable, and rock-like as the beautiful self in which it is supposedly grounded:

Lysander: The course of true love never did run smooth,
But either it was different in blood—
Hermia: Oh, cross! Too high to be enthralled to low.
Lysander: Or else misgraffed in respect of years—
Hermia: Oh, spite! Too old to be engaged to young.
Lysander: Or else it stood upon the choice of friends—
Hermia: Oh, Hell! To choose love by another's eyes.

The last line is truly delectable. Hermia is about to be plunged into that hell which she dreads, not by the hand of uncomprehending friends, not by an avaricious guardian or a reactionary father but by her own volition and most ardent desire. Later on, Hermia and her friends will make fun of *Pyramus and Thisbe* because of its crudeness but it is really *their* play, the only kind of play they can "understand," the play of a love thwarted by outside obstacles, a wall and a lion, as superficially insurmountable and terrifying as they are ultimately reassuring; reassuring for desire itself, which would be very much shaken if it had to acknowledge itself as its own worst obstacle.

The wall and the lion of *Pyramus and Thisbe* are about as responsible for the lovers' plight as the fairies were a little before, or the ass-headed monster, as responsible, no doubt, as the contemporary family's "repressiveness" for the long midsummer night of our youth's discontent. Behind outside obstacles and solid differences, we sense a deeper misunderstanding, a more radical confusion which no one wants to clear. The wall of misunderstanding must stand, the lion must keep roaring unintelligibly, Pyramus and Thisbe must die if we are to experience that "pity and fear" which is tragedy's "duty" to provide. Tragedy, obviously, is another accomplice of that desire which turns itself into walls, reactionary fathers and ass-headed monsters in order to remain invisible. Tragedy is an endless illustration of *The course of true love never did run smooth.*

Like the folk festival, like *A Midsummer Night's Dream* itself, tragedy has a cathartic resolution. Consolidation of Difference is the aim, through the same violent distortion as always. Tragedy is much more conspicuous than comedy or even the folk festival with its expulsion of "evil spirits." Collective violence is still plainly visible in tragedy. It provides the genre with its most essential feature, the tragic demise of the hero. Aristotelian "pity and fear" really mean that only crocodile tears are shed over the hero's death. Far from probing the riddle of that death, when we curse the *caprice* of the gods, or lament the injustice of *destiny,* we accept unquestioningly the verdict of collective violence. Tragedy brings the citizens closer to each other at the expense of the scapegoat-hero.

All figurative uses of the word catharsis go back to Aristotle's description of tragedy. Catharsis means purgation by violent means; the expulsion idea is still visible behind the reassuring pharmaceutical context. This context itself becomes less reassuring when we think that pharmacy goes back to *pharmakos,* the Greek word for certain misfits and maladjusted individuals whom the city of Athens nourished gratuitously, "raised," so to speak, and kept in reserve for the periods of trouble, when they were turned into human scapegoats. . . .[3]

We can guess, now, why Shakespeare placed *Pyramus and Thisbe* at the end of such a play as *A Midsummer Night's Dream.* We had catharsis before, not once, but twice, in a sense; first, the folk festival, then Theseus; now *Pyramus and Thisbe.* We are in catharsis up to our ears, if I may say, plenty of blood and gore, without the slightest admissible justification. This catharsis to end all catharses undermines itself and the episode becomes a satire not of "wretchedness o'er-charged," as Hippolita feared—and Theseus was correct to reassure her on that score—but of tragedy as a genre, of the whole theater, perhaps of language itself.

Without, as well as within the play, we have two levels of understanding once more. But they do not parallel each other. In order to be *really* understood, the comments of Theseus must be detached from their ostensible object which is the ridicule of the spectacle at hand.

As Theseus, for instance, appears to poke fun at the strangely worded announcement of the play, shall we deny that he is saying much more?

> "A tedious brief scene of young Pyramus
> And his love Thisbe, very tragical mirth."
> Merry and tragical! Tedious and brief!
> That is, hot ice and wondrous strange snow.
> How shall we find the concord of this discord?

In the speech on *degree* and elsewhere, the tragic genius of Shakespeare consists, perhaps, in suggesting the concordant nature of discord (*each thing meets in mere oppugnancy*) as well as the discordant nature of concord. Without degree, Ulysses says, we could not even name right and wrong. Language itself is Difference and justice is no more, and no less. Thus, the arm that holds the symbolic scales is never straight. Human justice is *lame* by definition.

It is true, indeed, that the essential conflict, the conflict of the tragic brothers, must at all costs be solved if men are to live together, and yet, it can receive only arbitrary solution.

How shall we find the justice of this injustice? Tragic language suggests the impossible dilemma but does not formulate it. Ulysses remains solidly on the side of Difference, like his worst enemies. *A Midsummer Night's Dream* goes further. Only in such veiled satire, can the poet "shake degree" to the point where its cathartic inviolability is questioned. The identity of violence as the cure and violence as the ill, of *degree* as sacred hierarchy and *degree* as an impure object of rival desires, is cryptically pointed out: *That is hot ice and wondrous strange snow.* If tragedy keeps evading the real question, *How shall we find the concord of this discord?*

At this level, we cannot dismiss as hyperbolic, or as mere aristocratic disdain of the arts, the following remark on tragedy:

The best in this kind are but shadows, and the worst are no worse if imagination amends them.

Can the theater give up *the course of true love never did run smooth;* can it give up placing the blame for love's roughness on "Wall, that vile Wall which did these lovers sunder?" Can the theater move away from its cathartic drug without shaking itself out of its mind, literally, as it keeps shaking degree? A modern question, indeed; but nothing is changed when the theater tries to unleash the violence it was formerly supposed to contain. Nothing is changed when, in order to save Oedipus, the rest of mankind must be expelled and the horrors of the Theban mythical plague are conjured up against all of us, which is literally what Artaud, both terrifying and naive, is trying to do in his *Le Théâtre et la peste.* The roar of the lion has become deafening. The lion may well eat all of us before he last "eats up himself." Are we sure we want the lion to have the last word?

If we want theater to go beyond catharsis, the only way is Shakespeare's way. Shakespeare's way in *Hamlet,* for instance, the tragedy which undermines its own tragic language, Shakespeare's way in *A Midsummer Night's Dream,* where the cathartic drug flows so freely that it becomes its own caricature and its own critique.

Language, here, does not mean the opposite of what is meant by the other speaker; it means more and beyond: *Oh, Hell! To choose love by another's eyes.* The lie is so beautiful that it *is* the truth, not through a pun, not through a "Freudian slip" or even the *Verneinung,* however much it may look like it, but through the characters' constant mistaking of what is theirs as others' and what is others' as theirs, through their constant misjudging of the different for the same, and the same for the different. To interpret correctly, all it takes is a little re-arranging. The interpreter must unite what language separates, separate what language unites. When the entire discourse of the four lovers is considered globally, after everything has been said, interpretation becomes a problem of *misplaced punctuation.*

When Quince recites his badly punctuated prologue, it may be doubted that the farce has no end but itself. Shakespeare is paving the way for Theseus' comment, a little too flatly pertinent on the literal level not to be read as the extraordinary statement that it is, on language as a mask of desire, on the completeness, that is, of the mixed-up configuration of that language:

His speech was like a tangled chain—nothing impaired but all disordered.

Shakespeare's radical critique of language smacks curiously

René Girard

of some contemporary "heresies," and yet it does not make him a man of our nihilistic age. It is we, strangely enough, and not he, unsurpassed master of words that he is, who believe that language is everything, even as it is nothing. Obviously eager not to be misunderstood on that point, Shakespeare has Theseus tell his wife, in a passage devoid of irony, that he has seen the most learned men remain speechless in his presence, unable to go through with their prepared sentences, but never was he, Theseus, deceived as to their true sentiments. It is moving to hear that language is nothing next to love—love, that is, in a sense that is not Lysander's— in the midst of a striking feat of language such as *A Midsummer Night's Dream.* Love may well be deserted by language, reduced to silence, even denied and betrayed; in the end, it does not matter because love needs no language at all to be understood, and to *understand:*

> . . . Trust me sweet,
> Out of this silence yet I picked a welcome,
> And in the modesty of fearful duty
> I read as much as from the rattling tongue
> Of saucy and audacious eloquence.
> Love, therefore, and tongue-tied simplicity
> In least speak most to my capacity.

STATE UNIVERSITY OF NEW YORK—BUFFALO

NOTES

1. "Symétrie et dissymétrie dans le mythe d'Oedipe," *Critique,* 249 (February 1968), 99-135.

2. *Ibid.,* pp. 120-35.

3. In *La Pharmacie de Platon (Tel Quel,* 1968), Jacques Derrida has studied the uses of *pharmakos* and its cognates, as well as the implications of these uses, in the works of Plato.

THE FUTURE OF PSYCHOANALYTIC CRITICISM

Edward Wasiolek

I

In a short essay at the beginning of this decade Norman Holland asked the following provocative question about the relationship between psychoanalytic criticism and New Criticism:

Some day, when the intellectual history of this century is written (by what amoebas or opossums?), one of the great puzzles will be, Why did two disciplines so closely related in methods and interests as New Criticism and psychoanalysis stand so long apart? A few critics, among them Edmund Wilson, William Empson, and Kenneth Burke, brought psychoanalysis proper into their criticism early and well. There are more now, Leon Edel, Leslie Fiedler, Lionel Trilling, Gordon Smith, Simon Lesser, Louis and Selma Fraiberg, and others writing for the important, but still little, little magazine *Literature and Psychology*. Nevertheless, most New Critics have ignored psychoanalytic criticism, so that New Criticism and ignored psychoanalytic criticism rest uneasily like two momentarily divided but potentially dangerous chunks of plutonium.[1]

Professor Holland's astonishment may be astonishing to some. For there are reasons, numerous and compelling, why psychoanalytic criticism and New Criticism have had little to do with each other. Psychoanalytic criticism has concerned itself with meaning, biography, content; New Criticism, with structure, language, and the inner workings of a work of art. New Criticism held undeviatingly to the principle that the critic was not to go beyond the text itself; psychoanalytic criticism invited the reader to speculate on the life of characters before and outside the text. New Criticism was concerned with separating art from life and psychoanalytic criticism with identifying art and life. When the disagreement was this wide on such an important and basic premise, it is not surprising that the two movements have had little to do with each other.

What may be surprising is that two movements so different should have arisen and flourished in the same era. Flourish is perhaps too strong a word for psychoanalytic criticism. Psychoanalytic criticism had a brief popularity of an off-beat sort in the twenties, but it has struggled against the tide and the critical establishment ever since. There is, of course, a formidable bibliography of psychoanalytic criticism, but much of it has been written by medical men and by uninfluential critics. Of those mentioned in Norman Holland's quotation only Lesser and Fraiberg have written extensively on psychoanalytical criticism and maintained a consistent commitment to a psychoanalytic point of view in their practical criticism.

New Criticism, on the other hand, did flourish and engage the best contemporary critical minds for more than a generation. It dominated the little magazines, the academic journals, and eventually the classrooms. Its gospel is still being spread by scores of young teachers who were trained in the methods and habits of the forties and the fifties. Psychoanalytic criticism, for the most part, was forced to find its way in medical and technical journals, and *Literature and Psychology* did not claim enough support for a long time to command the type of regular printing. If it entered the classroom, it did so surreptitiously, and even today literature and psychology are not boldly taught at many universities.

The New Critics engaged the proponents of other critical tendencies in serious dialogue: they argued with the literary historians most of all, briefly with the moralism of Ivor Winters, and energetically with the Chicago neo-Aristotelians. But to my knowledge they never engaged their most formidable opponent in a serious methodological argument. The grounds for a serious methodological discussion were there and are still there. Despite the distinctly different approaches that each took to the literary artifact, they touched at points in significantly interesting ways, and in ways that have not been sufficiently discussed. Both New Criticism and psychoanalytic criticism looked upon the poetic statement in ways that bore some similarity. In the later "contextualist" phase of New Criticism, the poetic statement became self-sustaining, impervious to paraphrase, invulnerable to irony, and self-reflexive. These extreme formulations grew out of assumptions made by I. A. Richards in the twenties. In *Science and Poetry* I. A. Richards made the distinction between propositional statements, which were about the world and found their model in science, and "pseudo-statements," which were not about the world and found their model in poetry. For I. A. Richards pseudo-statements pointed to the poet's feelings and experience, but for Cleanth Brooks the poetic statement pointed neither to the world nor to the poet's feelings. The context in later New Criticism was closed at both ends. Anyone who has read even randomly in the critical literature of the late forties and fifties knows how often and how incessantly theoretical discussions by New Critics had to do with distinctions of this sort.

We are accustomed to think of psychoanalytic criticism as concerned almost exclusively with content, yet the psycho-analytic view of poetic statements has interesting similarities to New Critical practice and theory. The poetic statement is not self-sustaining and self-reflexive for the psychoanalytic critic, but it is also not a generalization about the world in the usual referential sense. The generalizations a character makes in a novel or a play are often generalizations that serve as defense formations, the purpose of which is to keep specific painful meanings from rising to consciousness. We generalize about the world to protect ourselves from ideas that are painful or unpleasant to us. The very process of generalization raises personal and specific truths to universal and impersonal statements, thereby divesting the specific truth of personal responsibility. Surely, much of Hamlet's commentary on the unprofitability of the world and the times being out of joint are defense universals for what he suspects is wrong within himself, as Raskolnikov's self-flattering conception of himself as an extraordinary man hides a less flattering conception of himself as an inferior man.

Both psychoanalytic criticism and New Criticism reject the poetic statement as a simple commentary on the philosophical state of the world. Both are aware of the contextual complexity of the statement, one pointing to the personal and hidden drama of character, and the other to the linguistic complexity of the poetic statement. There is a further resemblance. Both psychoanalytic criticism and New Critical theory see the poetic statement as charged with multiple meaning. The psychoanalytic term for this is "overdetermination." Ideas in dreams, fantasies, and by extension ideas in art, carry often more than one psychic idea in condensed form. The New Critical terms for this phenomenon have been various: ambiguity, plurisignification, paradox, irony, and many others. Mere complexity, which to many seemed to be the end that was championed by Brooks and others, is never the end for psychoanalytic "overdetermination." The overdetermined idea, when unraveled, leads by way of specific association and by way of layers of defenses and through layers of repressed material to the hidden feelings, thoughts, and motivations of the speaker.

Despite these areas of general concern and of practice, there has been little recognition of common theoretical and practical problems. The Freudians arrived at the wrong historical juncture. While the New Critics were riding the crest of formalist sentiments, not only here but also abroad, the Freudians were reviving the very concerns that criticism had tired of: content, meaning, psychologizing, and biography. Even more they were reviving them in a form that drove many good critics into indifference and invective.

II

Psychoanalytic criticism has not constituted a bright episode in the history of twentieth-century criticism. The methodology has often been sloppy, the claims have often been exaggerated, and the conclusions have sometimes been outrageous. We have been treated to paradings of technical jargon, often irrelevant and seldom illuminating, to simple schematisms based on Freud's topography of the psyche, and to arbitrary patterns of symbolism. When a distinguished critic of Faulkner's novels tells us that Benjy in *The Sound and the Fury* represents the "Id," Quentin the "Ego," and Jason the "Super-ego," we may either yawn or we may rage, but we do not learn. When another critic tells us that Raskolnikov is a latent homosexual aching for Razumikhin, Luzhin, Svidrigaylov, Porfiry, and virtually every male char-

acter in *Crime and Punishment,* a useful psychoanalytic concept has been driven past usefulness.[2] And when a clinical
analysis of Dostoevsky results in the following, Freud's
provocative suggestions about Dostoevsky's character have
been transplanted into unprofitable jargon. Dr. Paul C.
Squires sums up his analysis of Dostoevsky's character in the
following way:

> Our formal diagnosis runs as follows: Dostoevsky was an
> epileptic schizophrene, paranoid type, complicated by
> hysterical overlay, *the epilepsy being foundational;* all
> the available data, including pictures of the man, point
> to an endocrine abnormality of which the chief com-
> ponents are hyperthyroid, hyperpostpituitary, and
> hyperparathyroid. *Dostoevsky was essentially a pituitary-
> centered individual.* His alcoholic and epileptoid heredity
> is outstanding.[3]

Dr. Squires's last comment is the following: "Unquestion-
ably, Fyodor Dostoevsky takes first place among the 'higher
degenerates' in the history of literature and art."[4]

Nor is one encouraged by progress in psychoanalytic criticism. In a book published in 1968, Normal Holland, one of
our most prolific writers on the subject, provides us with a
methodology of analyzing imagery in art from a psychoanalytic point of view. Such methodology would consist of
looking for oral, anal, urethic, and phallic imagery. By anal
imagery he means the following:

> As for imagery, one finds in anal writings a preoccupa-
> tion with dirt, with smells, particularly those which
> evoke disgust, and then with their transformations: fog,
> mist, sweet smells, pure air, light, even, ultimately,
> *logos,* the word of God. By this mechanism of "displace-
> ment upwards," the ear may come to stand for the
> anus—sounds are common anal images. The child-in-us

may consciously fantasize that insemination takes place by fluids or air or words entering the ear (as in various paintings of the Annunciation analyzed by Ernest Jones). Anal fantasies tend to stress laws and rules, particularly meticulous, precise, petty behavior, which deals especially with collecting or excessive cleanliness or rituals. Control, either by oneself or by another, is an important theme.

Another theme of anality is doing things in time: thus, impatience, procrastination, or things running by fits and starts would suggest that we are dealing with an anal fantasy, as would a concern with precise timing.[5]

These examples are not very special. They are almost the norm, and the norm has driven large portions of the academic and literary community to condemn psychoanalysis as a respectable literary procedure. And yet many of these same critics will acknowledge psychoanalysis as a revolution in our thinking about ourselves and an illumination of large areas of human behavior and motivation. The contradiction is tantalizing and bewildering.

As critics we cannot avoid talking about human behavior, feelings, motivations, and conceptualizations. Psychoanalysis has something to say about how we think, feel, generalize, and act; why we feel tired and how we handle anxieties; how we love and what happens to us when we stop loving. If we do not use the processes and conclusions of psychoanalysis in discussing these things, we run the risk of condemning ourselves to repeating the facile and erroneous generalizations of a pre-psychoanalytic age or run the greater risk of spinning out our own arbitrary psychologisms.

We can generalize about love in a facile and conventional manner, or we can use Freud's theory of narcissism and his explanation of how self-love is displaced but never replaced. We may have known before Freud that we do not love and hate with impunity, but it was Freud who traced out the mechanisms and logic by which the abandoned love object is reinstated in the self, there to suffer in self-punishment the aggressive component of every love relationship. Freud's comments on aggressiveness—which held equal status with the sexual drive in his later years—are brilliant in the number and sharpness of insights. It is from Freud that we have learned that one can commit suicide, not because the times are out of joint and not because one hates oneself, but because one hates someone else, that guilt can be the cause of crime as well as its consequence, that what we revere and what we abhor have the same source, that we can castigate ourselves when we lose someone in death not because of guilt, but from aggressiveness toward the departed, that saint-liness may lead to self-aggression, and repression of aggres-siveness to increase of self-aggression.

Freud has given us a new logic of behavior in which what we say may not be what we mean, and what we think may serve not elucidation but only defense. We have known for a long time that we will lie when our interests are threatened, that we give to others what we fear in ourselves, and that we defend ourselves when we are threatened. But never until Freud and psychoanalysis have we understood the extent and complexity of the individual's defenses against what is pain-ful and what he thinks is painful. He has taught us that the past exists not only in memory but also presently in the body. We act out in pantomime what we do not understand, and psychological offshoots of repressed and painful materi-als reach out to move our gestures and bend our tongues. We live in private and public worlds. What is more important, Freud has done more than perceive paradoxes—literary men have done that before him—he has explained them. He has with care and clarity fitted concept to concept, adjusted cause to cause, and brought fact to theory and theory to fact. It would seem strange indeed that literary critics who are called upon to generalize about human motives, feelings, aggressions, persecutions, love, hate, self-love, and depressions can afford to ignore the enormous body of specific insight and explanation that Freud and his followers have left us.

Nor does the possible usefulness of psychoanalytic insight stop with the analysis and expression of the individual psyche. Much of what Freud wrote and thought has important implications for the nature and purpose of art. One of the oldest problems of literary theory stems from the fact that some forms of art transmute painful content into pleasurable expression. We are accustomed to explaining this mystery by the mitigating influence of form, by aesthetic distance, and by the consciousness on the part of the audience that the terrible facts are not real. For Freud's conception of the repetition compulsion may have something to offer to our vocabulary and our understanding. One of the basic impulses of the child is to master painful situations by recreating them over and over again, so that by such recreation he can understand and master what is painful and threatening, and by such mastering render the painful matter harmless and even pleasurable.

There is even a fruitful analogy to be pursued between Freud's therapeutic aim and the function of art for the artist. Whatever else he is doing, the artist is dredging up what is inside him, externalizing it, and formalizing it; he raises what is inside him to consciousness where he may contemplate and confront it. This is similar to Freud's therapeutic goal, in which in the process of transference during the latter stage of a cure the patient raises to consciousness what he has resisted knowing. Transference is a kind of dramatization and contemplation of what has gone on inside oneself. What one was possessed by, one now possesses.

Dream work, too, is in many respects similar to the kind of logic that obtains in a literary work. In both dream and art the representation of the world is "picture," and in both logical relations become spatial, recalling perhaps the New Critical insistence on the iconic quality of poetry and perhaps even to the Jamesian insistence that picture and scene are the essence of dramatic and novelistic art. In dream work spatial relations like contiguity, succession, transformations, and order take the place of such logical relations as cause and effect, comparison and contrast, and either-or relations. Both dream and art seem to be a retranslation of a world sorted out by logic back into a more primitive mode of apprehension and perhaps a fuller apprehension of the world's body.

The use of dream symbolism or the interpretation of detail on the analogy of dream symbolism has been the most frequently criticized part of psychoanalytic criticism. The criticism has come from what seems to be the arbitrary and farfetched connections that psychoanalytic critics make between the literal detail and its symbolic significance. But what strikes us as farfetched in psychoanalytic symbolism is not farfetched if one understands psychoanalytic theory. The neurotic for Freud reveals his inner world in his gestures, words, actions, but the interpretation of these gestures is oblique, associative, and different from our ordinary way of interpreting. The interpretation of symbols, as usually conceived, is conceptualized so that we expect some logical, conventional, or material relationship between the symbol and the object symbolized: the symbol may be conventional like the cross or the rose; or it may be synecdochical like the square and hammer for a trade, or the symbol may partake of the nature of the thing symbolized. But psychoanalytic symbolism operates according to a different logic. The symptom or the substitute formation—in life and in dream— may be something remote in character from the thing it symbolizes; indeed by the very logic of psychoanalysis it would have to be remote and hidden, because the substitute formation is permitted expression precisely because it has been sufficiently displaced from what it has been substituted for. Something trivial may be important and something remote very near. The basis for such symbolic relationships lies in the fact that substitute formations and symptoms, which are our clinical analogy to symbolic detail, are screens for what is symbolized. Between them and what is symbolized may intervene layers of repressive psychic offshoots, so that the distance between the substitute formations and the symbolized material may be very great. The symbol, psychoanalytically speaking, does not willingly reveal what it points to. It conceals what is symbolized, and the path back to the symbolized matter may be very oblique and circuitous. When psychoanalytic criticism gives us the connection between the substitute formation and the symbolized material, it is likely to strike the reader as arbitrary and farfetched, because the intervening associative steps have not been revealed. The connections are not arbitrary because they are supported by clinical evidence and a coherent theoretical structure. But psychoanalytic critics have the obligation to spell out the methodology of interpretation in a refined way, to tell us by what methods and rules they derive their symbolizations.

III

The implications of psychoanalysis for literature even today seem immense, and yet it is clear that psychoanalytic criticism has failed to translate a vast body of specific clinical insight about human behavior into specific analytic tools for literary criticism. The reasons for the failure are many and complicated, but the reductive nature of much of psychoanalytic criticism has something to do with the failure. Psychoanalytic criticism seems to have condemned itself to tedious uncoverings of oedipal complexes, oral and anal fixations, and equally monotonous chartings of works according to Freud's psychic topographies. Preponderant attention has been paid to a few rather abstract and unitary concepts and too little to Freud's body of specific clinical data.

But reductionism can only be partly responsible for the failure. Reductionism is a hazard of any critical procedure, a fact that is often forgotten by the critics of psychoanalytic criticism. I doubt that we have had much more of it in psychoanalytic criticism that in certain forms of social, philosophical, and theological criticism. Even formalist modes of criticism can be reductive and indeed often are. The probability is that the tendency of psychoanalytic criticism to see all literature, no matter how different in form and nature, as uniform and invariable exemplifications of Freudian concepts has brought more discredit to psychoanalytic criticism than any other factor. We may be ready to admit that certain works or certain portions of works lend themselves to Freudian analysis, but psychoanalytic criticism seems to act at times—from arrogance to stupidity—with the view that all works must lend themselves to interpretation along these lines. It is the inflexibility and invariability of the procedure that many of us find offensive. It is the inability or unwillingness of psychoanalytic critics to find limits of application for their procedures that has alienated many potential sympathizers and has contributed more than anything else to the failures of psychoanalytic criticism.

The justification for the universal applicability of psychoanalytic principles is not hard to find. Psychoanalysis is a universal explanation of human behavior, and it defines a core of human nature that is beyond history and culture. If then—the argument runs—human motives and feelings in art are like those of life, then it must follow that psychoanalytic principles are at work in the feelings and actions that are portrayed and expressed in all works of art. However plausible the universal application of psychoanalytic principles may be in life, we feel instinctively that some distinction has to be made in art. Art is and it is not life. It is life selected, formed, and artificialized. Psychoanalysis may underlie all human behavior, but may not underlie a particular artistic representation of human behavior. The artist may be ignorant of the universal springs of human behavior; psychoanalysis may be wrong; the particular artistic representation may concern itself only with the symptoms and psychic offshoots of the deepest springs of human behavior; culture and history may so screen the deepest motives that the artist himself may consciously or unconsciously be capable of representing only remote substitute formations. In any event psychoanalytic critics have an obligation to concern themselves with what the artist has actually represented and not with what the psychoanalytic universals decree. We have no right to translate every representation of human behavior back into correct psychoanalytic theory.

The future of psychoanalytic criticism will be determined in part by the success or failure on the part of psychoanalytic critics in finding criteria of limitation of applicability of psychoanalytic principles. If we are to find such criteria, it would be good to find them in psychoanalysis itself. The oedipal complex, for example, is universal in the sense that every individual must pass through certain biologically determined stages, the most important of which is the phallic stage and along the path of which the individual may be "fixated," that is, may fail to develop normally to the next stage. The oedipal stage is the most important of childhood aetiology, the most difficult to pass through successfully, and, in Freud's opinion, very few of us pass through it with complete success. That is, the feelings of sensuous attraction for the parents, the ambivalence to the other, the feeling of fear and terror before the threat of castration, and the severe repression of what we fear is forbidden stays with us all our life and can be recathected in situations of stress and trauma. But it is not always recathected; it is not always manifest; it does not always have a decisive or even an important influence on an individual's behavior. The chances are that my oedipal complex lies quiescent when I'm playing tennis or watching a movie, or dining out, or engaging in numerous other situations. Or to put it more broadly, we may all be in some degree neurotics, since somewhere along our development, we have passed through the aetiology of childhood with some difficulty and hence retain some predisposition to fixation. But regressions to these points are not occurring all the time, but only in very specific circumstances.

There is a difference in psychoanalytic theory between an oedipal complex that is latent and one that is manifest. The distinction would seem to be simple, but it is seldom invoked in the application of psychoanalysis to literature. Psychoanalytic criticism, for instance, may look upon what a character says as not what he means; the expression may be any number of psychic defenses, projections, distortions of his real meaning. But, it need not be. What we say in life and in art may be what we mean. We defend ourselves against what is painful to our consciousness, and when we defend, we distort. But the unconscious and the conscious are not always in conflict. We cannot assume that there is always something hidden behind a character's words, that every generalization is intellectual projection, that every action is a gesture of defense against the pain of an inner world. Nor can we in psychoanalytic symbolizations assume that ladders are always indications of sexual intercourse; sometimes they are simply ladders. Ploughshares, hammers, guns, revolvers, daggers, and countless other pointed objects are not always penises. Freud himself warned against such indiscriminate symbolizings in psychoanalysis; the danger is even greater in literary criticism. One must distinguish between universal applicability, which may be true in theory, and specific circumstantial applicability, which must be true in practice.

I do not underestimate the difficulty of applying such a distinction to specific situations. How are we to know when an oedipal situation is manifestly present, and how are we to know that it is not. To make such a distinction, we will have to have what good critics must always have: judgment, knowledge, sensitivity, and patient observation. We will have to know psychoanalytic theory very well, too. When certain details are sufficiently insistent in a work of art, when they cluster—to use Kenneth Burke's term—about a situation that is sufficiently analogous to a psychoneurosis in the clinical sense, then we will be encouraged to entertain a psychoanalytic hypothesis. We may be encouraged to entertain a psychoanalytic explanation in situations where the motives given for an action are contradictory and numerous, as in *Crime and Punishment*; situations in which the events are structured as a series of evasions, as in Conrad's *Lord Jim*; or situations in which sexuality is manifest and an insistent part of the content. A large part of Faulkner's *The Sound and the Fury* is occupied explicitly with Quentin Compson's desires and inability to commit incest with his sister, and such a situation, I must maintain, permits the critic to entertain the possibility that psychoanalysis may throw some illumination on the feelings, motivations, and psychic wounds of Quentin. Cleanth Brooks in his study of Faulkner and his discussion of this novel never entertains such a hypothesis, and his reading of the novel leaves large portions of the novel opaque.[6] No one can read Act III, scene iv of *Hamlet,* where Hamlet confronts his mother in her bedroom, without noticing how compulsively Hamlet's mind attaches itself to one thing and to one thing alone: his mother's sexuality and his furious and frantic condemnation of her sexuality. No explanation of Elizabethan society, audience, or theater convention and no argument from Hamlet's general nature, no matter how refined, will help us explain the specific and manifest sexual relation between son and mother. Not even the murder of Polonius can divert him—except for a moment—from the flow of invective and sullied sexuality that he showers on his mother. He wants one thing and one thing alone and that is for his mother to desist from sleeping with his uncle and surrogate father. T. S. Eliot misread the play because he thought Gertrude was too trivial for the emotions she evoked in Hamlet. Psychoanalysis has taught us the obvious truth that no mother is trivial to her son.[7]

But unless a manifest situation is present in the literary work itself, sufficiently similar to the clinical data which defines a psychoneurosis, I do not believe we have the right to translate the behavior into the data of psychoanalysis. Psychoanalytic criticism must find its methodology of limitation and boundaries of responsible application, or its future will be met with as much abuse as its past practice. At the same time even where it may be legitimately applied to specific works, it does not have the automatic license to usurp to itself the function of being the sole valid mode of interpretation. *Hamlet* and *Crime and Punishment* have social and cultural dimensions, and we gain very little by dismissing them as simple rationalizations of psychological motivations. Some things are beyond culture, but not everything, and the form of psychoanalytic principles, if not the truths, varies a great deal with the culture. Freud himself pointed out that the oedipal situation was openly expressed in *Oedipus Rex,* but was hidden and repressed in *Hamlet.* [8]

There is nothing in the theory or practice of psychoanalytic criticism that militates, for example, against formalist or structural approaches to art. Russian formalism may have something to tell us about the "felt quality" of poetic language and the situational devices by which forms are deconventionalized and made poetic. The Chicago neo-Aristotelians may be able to tell us something about the emotional effect and the causative factors that bring about the effect; and various modes of New Critical contextualism may be able to tell us a great deal about how ordinary propositions may be nuclei of ambiguity, complexity, and paradox. And none of them—in doing these things—will be necessarily in conflict with psychoanalytic criticism. Ernest Jones's interpretation of *Hamlet* tells us something about Hamlet's relationship to his mother, father, and to Ophelia and his stepfather. But it doesn't tell us how the wrenching emotional effect of the play comes about; Chicago neo-Aristotelianism might be able to do that. And Jones's interpretation tells us very little about the inexhaustible well of linguistic expressiveness of the play; and New Criticism might tell us.

Psychoanalytic criticism is concerned primarily with what we ordinarily call "content," but analyses of content have implications for structure. How we read the motives of a Quentin Compson, a Hamlet, and a Raskolnikov changes numerous internal relationships in the work of art. What we see affects how we see. If a work of art consists of "formed content," and not just of form alone, and if a work of art takes its subject matter from life—and where else would it take it from—then psychological considerations, as well as social, religious, and philosophical considerations, are inevitably the concern of a critic. I cannot hazard what will be the concerns of criticism in the future, but I have an opinion about what needs revitalization in our critical lexicon. The content factor in our equation of "formed content" needs such revitalization. Considerations of "content" or "subject matter" have been rigorously and systematically reduced to irrelevance by the dominant formalist modes of reasoning for almost half a century. We have no vocabulary to deal with "content," but we are tired of having content defined as some abstract and unreal summary of content, and then on that basis being told that it has nothing to do with art. Content can be refined or abstract, just as formal properties can be refined or abstract. Content affects form as much as form affects content. They are not the same as the clichés of formalism seem at times to suggest. They are inseparable, but they are conceptually distinct. Psychoanalytic criticism has fought a rear-guard action for the defense of content, that is, for the relevance of life to art. If psychoanalytic criticism can live up to the promise of Freud's brilliance and can divest itself of its own defenses and enter the main stream of literary criticism, it may have an important part of play in the future of literary criticism.

But psychoanalytic criticism has to find its place in the spectrum of critical approaches before this can happen, and what is just as important, the spectrum has to permit it to find its place. There has been enough good psychoanalytic criticism to temper our despair before the avalanche of bad criticism, and to give us intimations, if not of immortality, at least of promise. Freud himself was always sensible and illuminating in his remarks on art; Jones's work on Hamlet has established itself as a convincing reading of at least one aspect of the play; William Snodgrass has given us one of our best explanations of Raskolnikov's motives;[9] Simon Lesser has written a provocative and suggestive book on the relationship of fiction and the unconscious; [10] Kenneth Burke has often mixed psychoanalysis, sociology, Marxism, and grammar in an idiosyncratic but fruitful way; and Lionel Trilling has read Freud with sensitivity and addressed himself intelligently to some of the speculative implications of Freud's comments on art.

It now appears that the long-range influence of psychoanalytic criticism may be greater than the various modes of formalist criticism that engaged so powerfully our attention during the last generation. The excitement and freshness New Criticism brought to the forties and fifties have faded away. We have been taught for a generation to read closely, and it may take another generation to teach us to read broadly. We continue to read closely, but we are less comfortable with the artificialities and limitations of contextualism. Myth, religion, biography, and social concerns are beginning to engage our attention and critical sensibility. What was "extrinsic" is now beginning to appear to be "intrinsic." The condemned intellectualist disciplines continue to press their relevance upon us. I. A. Richards and his New Critical followers attempted to save poetry from science, but it appears now that we will have to save criticism by bringing back the science and the intellectualist disciplines that were so energetically and consistently excluded. In this respect psychoanalytic criticism may have an important role to play, for theoretically, at least, psychoanalytic criticism is based on a rigorous and carefully defined discipline, supported by clinical evidence and a coherent theoretical structure.

During the last three or four years a "nouvelle critique" has been developing in France, and it may be that we will have to look there for a way in which the accomplishments of New Criticism may be integrated with the continuing promise of "intellectualist disciplines" like psychoanalytic criticism. French "New Criticism" does not see the literary artifact as an entity sealed off from the advances of intellectual and scientific knowledge, but as a point of convergence of various modes of knowing. This is a sane and fruitful conception of art, and a conception that history seems to be driving us toward, whatever our theoretical reservations. Psychoanalysis is participating in the development of French "New Criticism," and it should participate in the continuing development of contemporary American criticism. If psychoanalytic criticism can find its limits of applicability and find new modes of transporting the accumulated and accumulating body of specific insight of psychoanalysis to literature, it has important contributions to make to criticism, and criticism has an obligation to let it make them.

NOTES

1. Norman N. Holland, "The Next New Criticism," *Nation,* 192 (April 22, 1961), 339-341.
2. Edna C. Florance, "The Neurosis of Raskolnikov: a Study in Incest and Murder," *Archives of Criminal Psychodynamics,* I (Winter, 1955), 344-396.
3. Paul C. Squires, "Fyodor Dostoevsky, A psychopathological Sketch," *The Psychoanalytic Review,* XXIV (October, 1937), 346-388.

4. *Ibid.,* p. 385.

5. Norman N. Holland, *The Dynamics of Literary Response* (Oxford, 1968), p. 34.

6. Cleanth Brooks, "Man, Time, and Eternity," *William Faulkner* (New Haven: Yale, 1963), pp. 325-348.

7. F. L. Lucas, *Literature and Psychology* (Ann Arbor, Michigan: Univ. of Michigan, 1957), p. 57.

8. Freud said in *The Interpretation of Dreams:* "Another of the great poetic tragedies, Shakespeare's *Hamlet,* is rooted in the same soil as *Oedipus Rex.* But the whole difference in the psychic life of the two widely separated periods of civilization, and the progress, during the course of time, of repression in the emotional life of humanity, is manifested in the differing treatment of the same material. In *Oedipus Rex* the basic wish-fantasy of the child is brought to light and realized as it is in dreams; in *Hamlet,* it remains repressed, and we learn of its existence—as we discover the relevant facts in a neurosis—only through the inhibitory effects which proceed from it." *The Basic Writings of Sigmund Freud,* trans. and edited by Dr. A. A. Brill (New York: Modern Library), p. 309. *The Interpretation of Dreams* was first published in 1900.

9. W. D. Snodgrass, "Crime for Punishment: the Tenor of Part One," *The Hudson Review,* XVII (Summer, 1960), 202-253.

10. Simon D. Lesser, *Fiction and the Unconscious* (New York: Random House, 1957).

SOME NEW DIRECTIONS IN
RUSSIAN LITERARY CRITICISM

Edward J. Brown

In this paper I will be concerned with the most recent developments in Russian literary criticism, the events of today and yesterday—unfortunately, I have no hard information about tomorrow. In order to place the events of today in clearer perspective I would like to conduct a brief excursion into the past, dwelling on historical moments which have left deep traces in the Russian critical consciousness. There is a pronounced strain in Russian literary criticism of what Berdyaev once identified as "asceticism." The critics who formed literary attitudes in the nineteenth as well as in the twentieth century had only a peripheral interest in literature itself. They tended to avoid aesthetic pleasure or aesthetic concern as they labored solemnly over the body of literature in order to extract from it lessons, ideas, enlightenment. Vissarion Belinsky did not profess a systematic theory of literature, but he held certain beliefs which remain fairly constant throughout his career: the literary process was "thinking in images," the literary content was "native and national characters truthfully presented," and the purpose of literature was to refine and educate. Belinsky made grotesque misjudgments, as we know, of authors who failed to meet his demands. He thought Turgenev's *Hunter's Sketches* belonged to the physiological genre; he welcomed Dostoevsky's *Poor People* as a contribution to the "national school" because of its interest in the urban unfortunate, but he could not follow Dostoevsky when that author revealed abnormal states of mind or created fantastic situations, as in *The Double* and *The Landlady*. Belinsky valued literature for purposes of his own. Pushkin's *Eugene Onegin*, for instance, furnished him with occasions for developing many of his own ideas about society, about women, about relatives, about family life, about egoists, about the younger generation. In the course of his wide-ranging digressions in those famous articles on *Eugene Onegin*, he seems occasionally to trip over the literary work itself, and when he does he is curiously helpless. Instead of analysis or commentary, he offers the reader long quotations from the poem: "You see," he seems to say, "literature is good for you; read it."

Chernyshevsky was by his own account a disciple of Belinsky and a continuer of his work, but we must note that Chernyshevsky, especially in his early articles on Tolstoy, attends to literary problems on a level of sophistication seldom reached by Belinsky, and remarkable for the year 1855 in any criticism. In those articles he analyzes literary method, identifies Tolstoy's concern with the "psychic process," and contrasts Tolstoy's procedures in psychological investigation with those of Lermontov and Pushkin. As Professor Struve has pointed out, he invented and used for the first time in literary history the term "interior monologue." He came close to identifying the technique known later in Russian literary criticism as *skaz*. But Chernyshevsky soon put literary criticism behind him in order to give his energies as a writer to the propogation of social messages. His young friend and follower Nikolai Dobroliubov replaced Cherny-shevsky in 1957 as literary critic of the *Sovremennik.*

This might have seemed at first a step in the direction of specializing and dignifying the work of the literary critic, for Dobroliubov was both brilliant and erudite, and he had a flair for literature. He wrote with sensitivity on old Russian litera-ture, on eighteenth century Russian literature. He wrote the best article that has yet appeared in Russia on the critic and philosopher Stankevich, an article which curiously enough defends the gentle and contemplative philosopher against the crude call for action; he produced rhymed and unrhymed satirical pieces; he wrote lyric poetry which has more than historical interest. Yet Dobroliubov too, when he saw clearly the alternatives offered—sticking to his last as a critic or speaking out on urgent questions of social import—when he had to choose between aesthetic analysis and necessary labor—"did violence," as Apollon Grigoriev put it, "to his own love of art." To paraphrase Mayakovsky, he "stepped on the throat" of the literary critic in himself, and wrote that series of articles for which he is famous, articles on the vices of upperclass liberalism ("What is Oblomovism?"), on the need for active revolutionaries ("When Will the Real Day Come?"), on the oppression of the individual in Russian society ("A Ray of Light in the Kingdom of Darkness"). In each case a particular literary work furnished the pretext for developing an idea. Goncharov's *Oblomov,* Turgenev's *On the Eve,* Ostrovsky's play *The Storm* were texts for revolutionary sermons.

Chernyshevsky and Dobroliubov were only mild ascetics in comparison with Dmitri Pisarev, who rejected artists in favor of cobblers or chemists or cooks, and who in his article, "The Destruction of Aesthetics" proposed not forty days and forty nights but an indefinite period of fasting in the wilderness. Pisarev's basic relief was that Russia could not afford to expend intellectual energy on the production of aesthetic values. The natural sciences offered the chief hope for Russia, and writers might have a place in his "Republic" only if they contributed to the improvement of society. One need hardly point out that much of Soviet criticism of the "socialist realist" period sounds like a belated echo of Pisarev.

There were many other critics in the nineteenth century and even earlier, but Belinsky and the three "radical critics," Chernyshevsky, Dobroliubov, and Pisarev, have the most prominent place in the Russian literary consciousness. The attitude they represented toward literature and literary criticism has been artificially strengthened by official approval, huge editions of their works, and a multitude of books and articles about them. Their contemporary, Apollon Grigoriev, a critic who valued literature and attended to its problems, was a formidable opponent of the nineteenth-century radical critics and wrote with quiet scorn of their opaqueness to literature. But Grigoriev's works have never been published in anything like their full form, and an interest in his ideas has only recently revived in the Soviet Union. The symbolist critics, too, identified the indifference to literary values in the work of their predecessors of the mid-century, but neither are they prominent in the consciousness of contemporary critics. The Russian formalists placed literature itself in the focus of the critic's attention and members of that school—Jakobson, Eichenbaum, Shklovsky Tomashevsky—produced studies of literary form that are still alive today; but formalism was crudely suppressed in the late twenties and stigmatized as subversive.

Free consideration of various possibilities in the study of literature was discouraged in the Soviet Union after 1930 and a crudely simplified version of mid-nineteenth-century radical criticism, decked out in Marxist phrases, was installed as official dogma. And yet it is clear now that critical thought lived on in the underground. One is reminded here of the situation in nineteenth-century Russia that Alexander Herzen

commented on in his autobiography, *My Past and Thoughts.*
During an earlier period of repression, the reign of Nicholas I,
Herzen found evidence that intellectual life had continued
though the main arteries for its expression had been cut off.
"Future generations will wonder," he said, "at the emptiness
of this period [the 1830s] and will search for the lost
evidences of intellectual activity, which had in fact not been
interrupted. To all appearances the stream had been stopped,
Nicholas had tied up the artery; but the blood continued to
flow in bypaths. It is precisely this capillary flow which has
left its mark in the works of Belinsky, and in the correspondence of Stankevich."

My hope in undertaking this investigation was to find
evidence that in contemporary Russian literary criticism the
vital flow has not stopped; what I believe I have found is that
critical thought does continue and is frequently published,
even though it moves by indirection and along "bypaths."
Interesting evidence both of the restrictions on literary criticism and of its persistence in curious ways in spite of restric-
tion, was offered in a recent article by Professor Deming
Brown entitled "The Present Condition of Soviet Criticism."[1] Professor Brown set forth in ghastly detail the results
of his heroic researches in the literary journals. The main
body of critics seemed to him a well-disciplined and pon-
derous army manipulating with great assurance a limited
arsenal of sociological clichés. But Professor Brown's article
was followed in the same magazine by an interesting Post-
script which he wrote after he had made a trip to the Soviet
Union, as a corrective based on personal observation. He said
that in visiting the Soviet Union he was "reminded once again
of the huge lack of correspondence between what is printed
and what is believed." Professor Brown was convinced by his
talks with Soviet critics that the condition of literary criticism is more complex and at the same time more hopeful
than it appears when observed from outside the country. He

found evidence of general discontent. In fact it seemed to him that the conservative critics themselves were aware that they do not have the support of cultivated, intelligent, and sophisticated readers. There is an interesting historical analogy here with the situation of the 1830s described by Herzen, when the vital flow continued along the capillary bypaths of private correspondence, and private discussions among friends. What intellectuals say to one another, apparently, often has little relation to what is actually published in approved form.

Professor Deming Brown's article was followed early in 1967 by Nina Berberova's study of current Soviet criticism, which provided convincing evidence that the "discontent" noted in the earlier article had actually come to the surface in many ways.[2] One of the most interesting points of departure was the work of Franz Kafka, whose *Metamorphosis,* translated into Russian early in 1964, called forth a number of articles, not all of them routine performances of clichéd exorcism. The total effect of these articles was a kind of naturalization process: Kafka was granted a Soviet passport, conditional, it is true, and limited. His works were forced into the convenient Procrustean couch of orthodox "realism." After all, they do reflect life in a certain bourgeois milieu; and could it not be said that they "reveal the decay of bourgeois values" in Prague and Vienna? Amused condescension at this kind of thing would really be out of place; after the long breadless famine through which Russia had passed, one could be grateful, in 1964, even for stones.

Berberova's excellent article comments interestingly on a number of other events in the literary world that served as impulse to new ideas. The exchange program itself was in many ways an important catalyst. A symposium on the modern novel held in Leningrad in 1963 brought Soviet critics together with Western writers such as Sartre, Robbe-Grillet, and Natalie Sarraute in a discussion of the nature and function of literature. The critique of "realism" offered by the Western writers may have prepared minds for the idea that great literature might contain something more than "reflection of life" or approved moral lessons.

My own examination of the literary and scholarly magazines during the most recent period has revealed a number of new directions in which literary criticism and even more notably literary scholarship is moving. This movement has come about as a result of a pattern of interaction between literature and other disciplines, a kind of interaction which is not unknown in the West. Contributions to literary criticism have come from unexpected directions: from the natural sciences, from mathematics, from cybernetics, from the cinema, from the scholarly investigation of Old Russian literature, from the producers of bibliographies and reference works; and one of the most important sources of vitality is memoir literature and archival publications.

Let us look first at evidences of a beneficient contribution to literary criticism by the exact sciences. Literary critics have seemed at times to be consciously seeking assistance from disciplines which are well-organized and sure of their methods and their purposes. Literary criticism is admittedly a mess, and scholars may well be envious of their colleagues in physics and mathematics, whose terminology is pure of troublesome ambiguity and whose results can be quantified. The Soviet scientist inhabits a heaven from which literary scholars have been banished: the party imposes no program on physics and mathematics except the pragmatic one of getting results, and results in those fields have been sensational.

It is not surprising, then, to find in a recent number of the journal *Problems of Literature* an article by Kuznetsov, a historian of science, on "Dostoevsky and Einstein" which develops a parallel between the ideas of modern non-Euclidian physics and the behavior of a literary artist.[3] This article was accompanied in the same issue by an answer from one Mikhail Gus, an orthodox critic and propagandist, who, while pointing out the article's theoretical shortcomings, did accept it as an interesting contribution to literary discussion.

The article in question takes its departure from certain of Einstein's statements concerning Dostoevsky, statements to the effect that Dostoevsky had meant very much to him. Is there, then, an affinity between the great novelist and the great physicist? Kuznetsov maintains that Dostoevsky's poetics, that is, his literary procedures, were *rational* in spite of his seeming espousal of the irrational. However paradoxical and contradictory the emotions of his heroes, the actual experience of each one develops an idea. Moreover, many of his characters, and indeed Dostoevsky himself, are driven by a passion for experiment, at whatever cost to established moral truth. Stavrogin in *The Possessed,* for instance, is absorbed by a purely cognitive task: he wants to *measure* to what degree he himself or his partner can rise or fall in the moral scale. Dostoevsky as a propagandist, says the author, may have been satisfied with "Euclidian" answers to life's problems, but Dostoevsky the artist, in his experimentation with human nature, sought and was willing to accept unheard-of "non-Euclidian" ones.

Kuznetsov draws an interesting parallel between Einstein's rejection of the idea advanced in quantum physics that the particular and individual event cannot be predicted, and Ivan Karamazov's moral revulsion at the idea that no "law" applies to individual human cases but that in the ultimate statistic of the universe some kind of justice will be done. What may be involved here is that Einstein's moral ideals required a parallel morality in the harmony of the universe itself. One of the frequent thoughts thrown out incidentally by our scientist-critic is that throughout the work of Dostoevsky the point of contention and the point at issue is the individual human being: any final, impersonal, statistical harmony—in heaven, or, we might say, in the socialist society—must take into account local and miniscule events, the particular and the individual.

What is especially interesting about this study of Dostoevsky and Einstein is the experiment it offers in applying to the problems of literature the attitude and the approach of modern science: any moral, social, or literary phenomenon, the author seems to say, should be investigated experimentally without regard to fixed traditional forms of thought.

The field of mathematics has in recent years made an important contribution to the study of literature, particularly to the study of versification. The revival of interest in the application of statistical techniques to verse study began many years ago in the Soviet Union. Important stastical studies of Mayakovsky have appeared, and it is safe to say that this is the most important body of critical work on that poet yet produced in the Soviet Union. I have spoken of this as a revival. As a matter of fact Russian critics were early practitioners of the stastical method in the study of verse. The symbolist poet Andrei Bely, a trained mathematician, worked out as early as 1910 statistical patterns illustrating the individual modulation of a particular poet's line. The formalist critic Boris Tomashevsky, also a mathematician, applied mathematics to the study of verse in the 1920s. This early work has not been forgotten, and Russian critics have not lost the sense that they, after all, were early investigators in this field.

A widely respected professor of mathematics at Moscow University, M. Kolmogorov, has organized a circle of students and collaborators who investigate the problems presented by the verse of many poets, among them Pushkin and Mayakovsky.[4] The principal contribution of these studies, I think, is that they have placed the study of Mayakovsky on an objective footing. They are necessarily free of dogmatic clichés or

hagiographic obeisance, and they treat the poet as a phenomenon to be investigated, by scientific procedures which offer
quantitative results. And science, you know, is sacrosanct.
The upshot of this concentrated study has been a much
better understanding of Mayakovsky's particular poetic
genius as well as of the significance in context of characteristic quick shifts in his metrical patterns. In a 1964 article
Zhirmunsky[5] sums up and interprets the significance of the
work that has been done. Statistical analysis has revealed a
variety of metrical systems in the work of Mayakovsky: 1)
traditional syllabo-tonic meters; 2) free iambics or trochées
with lines of varying lengths; 3) regular accentual lines; 4)
irregular accentual lines (varying number of accents per line).
The raw results of the mathematicians have provided literary
scholars with interesting problems. One of these is the surprisingly high percentage of strictly traditional syllabo-tonic
lines, especially in Mayakovsky's earliest verse, but also in his
later and mature work. Examining the matter closely, Zhirmunsky is able to show that the use of purely conventional
meters by the mature Mayakovsky almost always has a poetic
function: the conventional beat tends to mark either styliza-
tion or parody. Where this explanation does not apply, Zhirmunsky suggests that the use of conventional meters in a
basic context of accentual verse sets up a kind of tension or
ambivalence: when the regular cadence of iambic or trochee
is introduced into a pattern of accentual lines this increases
the auditory variety and piques the curiosity of the hearer as
to both sense and form. The same effect is achieved by an
opposite procedure in the poem *The Sun,* where a regular
iambic beat is occasionally interrupted by surprising accentual lines. In sum then, mathematical analysis has helped to
illuminate Mayakovsky as a versifier, and suggested techniques for the study of other poets. And Zhirmunsky's article
offers a model of how a literary scholar may use the data
provided by statistical studies to illuminate the total sense of

a text. A volume recently published under the editorship of Zhirmunsky, among others, includes a number of articles that try to define objectively the notion of Russian "pausative" verse, along with articles dealing with syllabic verse and comparative metrics.[6] In a word, the mathematical analysis of verse forms is an established technique in the Soviet Union. Even the orthodox critic Timofeev accepts it.

A closely related development is the application to literary problems of the techniques and apparatus of cybernetics; and here too the most important result has been to introduce into a messy discipline—one dominated in the Soviet Union by dogma and cliché and practiced often enough by people obviously unqualified for serious study—something approaching scientific detachment and system. The literature on the subject of cybernetics is extensive; the bibliography is surprising in the range of topics treated, and as a branch of criticism this too would seem to be well-established.

An article by a French Communist in a recent issue of the authoritative journal *Kommunist* contains a ponderously favorable statement on structuralism and the work of Lévi-Strauss, and offers hopeful comment that the ideas advanced by this school are not necessarily "undialectical," and should be studied by Marxists.[7] In this area too it is not difficult to demonstrate a certain priority for Russians. A small but energetic group interested in structural poetics quite frankly traces its lineage to the early Russian formalists and claims as precedents for some of the work now being done such things as Propp's *Morfologiia skazki,* a study of the structure of folk tales in terms of situations and motifs, and Shklovsky's *Novella tain,* an analysis of all the Sherlock Holmes novels as a series of variations on a single basic plot.

The group interested in "structural poetics" has as yet published very few practical demonstrations of the method. Two of them (Zholkovsky and Shcheglov) quite frankly admitted in a recent joint article (*Problems of Literature,* No.

1, 1967, pp. 82 ff.) the dearth of structuralist criticism and attempted to remedy this lack by a structural analysis of one of the opening scenes in Ilf and Petrov's novel *Twelve Chairs.* This particular example is not encouraging. The authors take a relatively simple and straightforward episode (the auction of the chairs) and meticulously dissect it in terms of various devices, complicating the uncomplicated by dividing and subdividing these devices, and providing for it all a ponderously "exact" terminology: emphasis, opposition, contrast, intensification, equilibration, development, and so forth. Nevertheless, the discussions of structuralism, and the few examples of the method that have been published, seem an important breakthrough in that they have introduced the idea that literary works are the proper subject for objective study, just like other "natural" phenomena. The insistent presentation of this point of view may subtly undermine the once pervasive ideological and sociological approach to literature, and some writers explicitly reject the arbitrary imposition of ideological "schemes" or "systems" which pretend to give a final word on the nature and sense of literary works. The work of this group has clearly been influenced by Jakobson and Lévi-Strauss.

Another rich source of new and vital ideas is, surprisingly enough, the study of film-making. Fascinating commentaries on the film-making process have recently appeared, and there are available, if you look for them, some brilliant studies of particular films as well as of the relationship of the film structure to novel and story-making. In fact it may very well be that, as Berberova suggests, the surge of interest in modern Western literature during the last seven or eight years has been in part the result of contact with the Western cinema. We remember that Fellini's *8½* was awarded the first prize at a film festival in Moscow in 1963; there was much discussion of that film and many articles about it appeared. One of the most insightful and sophisticated discussions of Fellini that I have read appeared in 1965 in one of the volumes of a series called *Problems of Movie-Making.*[8] Let me quote briefly from that article some remarks on the opening scenes of the film *8½:* "Of course both of these scenes symbolize the tragic rift between freedom and nature on the one hand and the actual life of the individual human being in the contemporary West. These symbols are not only saturated with concrete meaning, they are *constructed* out of purely realistic, objective details taken from everyday life. The collision and contrast of major themes and different levels of action creates a peculiar aesthetic unity, within which, as in a fugue, we hear a number of distinct refrains.

Another article written somewhat earlier attempts to define the nature of the modern film in terms of what the author called "poetic and prosaic" methods. The "poetic" movie avails itself of "a new system of expression" demanding of the viewer intellectual effort and emotional involvement. On the other hand there is another kind fo film, she says, "narrative, prosaic, and two-dimensional." The author of this article, Turovskaia, makes it perfectly clear that in speaking of the distinctive features of a modern film she is actually discussing modern art as a whole.[9]

The reported experience of making movies and an increasing awareness of developments in the West in that art have, as we see, injected into Russian criticism the life-blood of new ideas. The critic Sarnov, for instance, is able to understand and explain Kataev's technique in his two autobiographical and confessional novels *The Holy Well* and *The Grass of Oblivion* as analogous to Fellini's cinematic practice in mingling various dimensions—spatial, psychological, and temporal.[10]

Another source of literary analysis is the published articles and diaries of the director Eisenstein. One of these deals interestingly with the relation of literature to the film and specifically with the problem of what kind of literature lends itself to the uses of the camera. Eisenstein compares Balzac and Zola as cinematic subjects and finds (in spite of the fact that Engels preferred Balzac) that Zola's scenes, because of their concreteness and particularity, because of the visual quality of the details in them, lend themselves more readily to cinematographic treatment.[11] This article and Eisenstein's other recently published writings are important for a number of reasons. They call in question heretofore unquestioned authorities not on ideological grounds but by invoking the concrete needs and procedures of a particular art, and they force the reader and the critic to attend to structure and form in the terms of a particular artist's problems.

Another bypath along which the vital fluid moves is the scholarly investigation of old Russian literature. Students of old Russian literature tend to be linguists or historians and one would not necessarily expect from them new discoveries in aesthetic analysis. Moreover, it is a well-established conviction—some would say a prejudice—that what remains of old Russian literature offers, with only a few exceptions, historical or linguistic rather than literary evidence. And yet, one of the most stimulating achievements in modern Russian literary criticism is D. S. Likhachov's recently published book *The Poetics of Old Russian Literature.* Important also is a recent article in which he treats the old question of the relationship between art and reality, advancing the thesis that literary works when they deal with space, time, and the material world behave according to their own internal laws so that no one-for-one correspondence can be found between the real and the artistic.[12] And he makes the relatively sophisticated point that even historical works *transform* reality and must be studied in terms of a particular author's purpose, system of views, and tendency. *A fortiori,* then, an admittedly artistic production, says Likhachov, refracts external reality in accordance with its own internal structure, the laws of its own functioning, and its own special sense.

The work of art actively transforms its material and therefore to treat a novel in two-dimensional fashion as a "reflection of reality" is to be grievously misled. The problem of time in literary works, a question that Likhachov realizes has been widely discussed in the West, he illuminates by bringing to bear on that problem the peculiar sense of a time linked to eternity which he finds in the medieval Russian chronicles. From that standpoint he is able to offer revealing definitions of the time sense to be found in a number of Russian novelists of the nineteenth century: the "chronicle" time of Dostoevsky, the even and slow-flowing time of Turgenev, the perennially "present" time of Goncharov. His contributions are a delight to read; they reveal many things in the novelists concerned that we had not seen clearly before. And while his critical method is not exactly a great discovery, it is a first-rate achievement in Russian literary criticism, and his book is one of the best evidences we have that independent and original thought about literature does go on in spite of rigorous environmental discouragement.

Encyclopedias, dictionaries, reference works—these too are a source of vitalizing ideas and original thought. We would not normally think of looking in encyclopedias for such things but that is exactly where you often find them in contemporary Russia. The recently published *Concise Literary Encyclopedia*[13] is an achievement, not only because it rehabilitates and discusses with decent objectivity scores of writers who were repressed or exiled or shot. What is most striking and surprising about this encyclopedia is that it is a source of unprejudiced information on a wide variety of literary topics. It has been attacked for just this reason but it is also being defended, and what has been written about it testifies largely to the high scholarly level of many articles, particularly those on modern developments in the arts and in literary criticism. Some of the articles are excellent by any standards, particularly those on literary theory, on the gro-

Edward J. Brown

tesque, on Hegel and Kant, on literature and mathematical method, Dostoevsky, Herzen. The tendency of these encyclopedia articles is to encourage the abandonment of the coarse simplicities that still dominate the literary world. The article "Literary Science" offers curious evidence that ideas widespread in Western Europe are not without effect in Russia and that the Lord—or something—"moves in a mysterious way his wonders to perform." The article offers one of the best short histories of literary criticism in Western Europe that I have found—and I suspect it owes much of its factual material to careful study of René Wellek's _History of Literary Criticism,_ which is given prominent space in its bibliography. The reader of this article will receive brief but serviceable information on the ideas of Bergson, Croce, Walzel, Eliot, I. A. Richards, Leavis, the New Humanists, the New Critics, Freud and his followers, Jung, Maud Bodkin, Northrop Frye, the structuralist critics, and many others, including the critics of the Chicago School. The article is a _tour de force_ in that it compresses vast information into a tiny space, and without falling into the reference work rut of merely listing names and books.

Another reference work that is alive with new ideas and approaches is a poetic dictionary authored by A. Kviatkovsky and published in 1966. [14] This work is an important phenomenon in the area of literary criticism for a number of reasons. First, it is the work of _one_ human being, and as such it is a feat of fantastic proportions considering the hundreds of entries. One would expect such a work, considering the importance of correct "definitions," to be produced by a collective presided over by a guardian of orthodoxy and operating with generally accepted literary criteria. But _one_ man did it, and he's not very orthodox. It is a curious performance. Critics have called it a "self-portrait," and accused the author of subjectivism, a word which in this case translates into "originality." The author seems indeed to be

184

almost oblivious of the existence of authorities, and he presents his definitions without obeisance and with a marked preference for his own ideas. All of the articles that deal with versification call in question the conventional terms and categories, in place of which Kviatkovsky proposes a system of his own which he calls tactological, and which derives the rhythms of poetry from the musical beat, dispensing with "outworn" and "mistaken" concepts such as iambic and trochaic. Kviatkovsky blandly calls in question the accumulated work on verse structure of all the authorities, beginning with Lomonosov and Tretyakovsky and ending with Zhirmunsky. I must admit that I think his versification theories are probably mistaken, but I find heartening the boldness with which he utters his new word on this subject.

Old archives and memoir literature are another source of new ideas. In fact one of the techniques used by liberal scholars to justify cautious and timid adjustments in the official attitude toward literature and the arts is the publication of material from the archives of Maxim Gorky, an unquestioned authority on literature. Gorky, as it turns out, admired Pasternak, Babel, Platonov, Bulgakov, and many other Soviet writers who were strangers to the practice of orthodox realism. There is no doubt that the massive publication of the Gorky archives undertaken in the sixties led to some curious results, for instance to the republication of Andrei Platonov and the appearance of Bulgakov's novel *Master i Margarita.* During the same time period the complete collection of the works of Lunacharsky appeared, and this voice from the past also had a liberalizing effect because Lunarcharsky was a sophisticated student of literature who at times defended futurists, Proletcultists, and formalists against Lenin's bigoted attacks. During the early twenties he attempted to mitigate the anathema being pronounced on the formalists, and even to modify somewhat the activities of the censorship. The opinions of Gorky, Lunacharsky, and Voronsky on many literary questions have seemed a revelation in the Soviet Union and have opened up an unsuspected range of possibilities even within the parameters of official Marxism.

Disciplines both remote from literature and contiguous with it are contributing unobtrusively to literary science. Among these disciplines we should not forget philosophy. Not only have first-rate articles on Hegel, on Maritain, and on Spengler appeared recently in literary journals, but a magnificent study of Dostoevsky, one of the best critical works on that novelist that has appeared anywhere, was published by a student of philosophy, one Ia. E. Golosovker, under the title *Dostoevsky and Kant.*[15] Golosovker constructs an intricate model of *The Brothers Karamazov,* analyzing that work as an extended commentary on the four Kantian antinomies. The latter are embodied in opposed characters, in their conflicting ideas, and in the verbal symbols associated with each one. This work is ingenious, subtle, immensely informed, and beautifully written.

Informed and subtle criticism is often inspired by artists whose works raise unorthodox questions. Kataev's recent experimental prose offerings were the occasion for an illuminating discussion of literary concepts, genres, and narrative procedures. Vladimir Gusev subtly discusses the "narrator" in *The Grass of Oblivion* and his function in that story, neatly identifying the devices by means of which the author conveys his ironical attitude to that narrator, who is indeed only himself, the author.[16]

Russian critics have recently come to understand that Russian literature was in the forefront of the movement in Europe which produced Joyce, Kafka, Proust, and in fact the whole host of moderns. An article entitled "Experimental Literature" points out that Pilniak, Bely, Andreev actually anticipated Western modernism, and the date of the completion of Pilniak's novel *The Naked Year* is given with solemn emphasis as "25 December 1920," in other words, two years before James Joyce's *Ulysses* and about the same time, as the author puts it, as Gertrude Stein's "extravaganzas." [17] We Russians, they say, "invented modernism and the anti-novel, we had our decadents before they did." Does this acknowledgement presage a more receptive attitude toward the modern accent in literature and literary criticism, or does the critic in question regard modern deviants from realism as an unfortunate survival of tendencies long since outgrown in the Soviet Union? The answer is not always certain, but depends on the context and the critic. At any rate Russian pride is certainly assuaged by the sense of early acquaintance with the difficult techniques of modern art as well as with structuralism, formalism, and mathematical poetics. And where national pride is operating, wonders may be wrought.

I hope I have conveyed in this essay some sense of the multiplaned variety of the Russian critical tradition in the nineteenth century as well as in the twentieth century. At the present moment many facets of that tradition are operating. One has to inspect the deceptively smooth surface long and carefully before detecting evidences of the energetic movement underneath. The tradition that still dominates is that of the radical critics, whose renunciation of literature was really a form of self-renunciation. But Marxist criticism, too, is still alive; there is a renewed interest in Plekhanov, Voronsky, and Lunacharsky; the work of Western Marxists is having some effect in Russian literary circles. Apollon Grigoriev has been republished and is widely read. Formalism is quietly revived among the neo-structuralists. All of this has happened incidentally, by the way, without explicit plan or intention, and as the result of the complex interaction of many intellectual disciplines with literary study. I have presented here the most interesting evidences I could find in my scouting of the bypaths. I would submit that the harvest is not inconsiderable and that Russian criticism, in spite of the inhibitions

Edward J. Brown

under which it labors, does find ways to speak its word about literature. And the intricate mechanisms by means of which that word is articulated and heard surely have interest not only for Kremlinologists and historians of culture but also, perhaps, for literary critics. At the moment there is evidence of increasing pressure toward conformity in Soviet intellectual life. Though it is impossible to foresee the future, the evidence presented here does. I submit, support the belief that the intellectual culture which has produced under difficulties so much interesting and original literary criticism will continue to survive.

NOTES

1. Deming Brown, "The Present Condition of Soviet Criticism," *Comparative Literature Studies,* I (1964), 165-173 and 325-326.
2. Nina Berberova, "Sovetskaia kritika segodnia (Soviet Criticism Today," *Novyi zhurnal,* December 1966, March 1967.
3. B. Kuznetsov, "Obrazy Dostoevskogo i idei Einsteina," *Voprosy literatury,* No. 3 (1968), 138-165.
4. Some of the more important articles in this field are the following: M. Kolmogorov, A. M. Kondratov, "Ritmika poem Majakovskogo," *Voprosy iazykoznaniia,* No. 3 (1962), 62-74; A. M. Kondratov, "Evoliutsiia ritmiki Maiakovskogo," *Voprosy iazykoznaniia,* No. 5 (1962), 101-108. V. Nikonov, "Ritmika Majakovskogo," *Voprosy literatury,* No. 7 (1958), 89-108.
5. V. Zhirmunskii, "Stikhoslozhenie Maiakovskogo," *Russkaia literatura,* No. 4 (1964), 3-26.
6. *Teoriia stikha,* edited by V. Zhirmunskii and others (Leningrad, 1968).
7. Guy Besse, "Rol' marksistko–leninskoi filosofii v ideologicheskoi borbe,"*Kommunist,* No. 8 (1968).
The following recent articles on structuralism are important: I. Revzin, "O tseliakh strukturnogo izucheniia khudoshostvennogo tvorchestva," *Voprosy literatury,* No. 6 (1965), 73-87; "Literaturovedenie i kibernetika" (a symposium), *Voprosy literatury,* No. 1 (1967), 73-123;

New Directions in Russian Criticism

"Literaturovedenie i kibernetika" (a symposium), *Voprosy literatury*, No. 10 (1967), 115-143; M. Kagan "Itak 'strukturalizm' ili 'antistrukturalizm' "? *Voprosy literatury*, No. 2 (1969), 113-135. Professor Berberova's article, referred to above, contains references to earlier articles on this subject (see, especially, *Novyi zhurnall*, No. 86 (March 1967), 124-127.

8. S. Korytnaia, "Kinogenichen li dukhovnyi mir?" in *Siuzhet v kino* (Moscow, 1965), 153-191.

9. M. Turovskaia, "Prozaicheskoe i poeticheskoe kino segodnia," *Novy Mir*, No. 9 (1962).

10. B. Sarnov, "Ugl pylaiushchii i kimval briatsaiuschchii," *Voprosy literatury*, No. 1 (1968), 21 ff.

11. S. Eisenstein, "Literatura v kino," *Voprosy literatury*, No. 1 (1968).

12. D. Likhachov, "Vnutrennii mir khudozhestvennogo proizvdeniia," *Voprosy literatury*, No. 8 (1968), 74-88.

13. *Kratkaia literaturnaia entsiklopediia*, Vol. IV (1967), Vol. V (1968).

14. A. Kviatkovskii (ed.) *Poeticheskii slovar* (Moscow, 1966).

15. Ia. E. Golosovker, *Dostoevskii i Kant* (Moscow 1963).

16. V. Gusev, "Dve storony medali," *Voprosy literatury*, No. 1 (1968), 52 ff.

17. P. Palievskii, "Experimentalnaia literatura," *Voprosy literatury*, No. 8 (1966), 78 ff.

NOTES ON CONTRIBUTORS

Edward J. Brown has been Professor of Slavic Languages at Stanford University since 1969. He was a member of the faculty at Brown and Indiana universities as well as Chairman of their Slavic departments. In addition to having been a Rockefeller, ACLS, and Howard Fellow, he was an exchange professor to the USSR in 1963. His principal publications include *The Proletarian Episode in Russian Literature* (1953), *Russian Literature since the Revolution* (1963), *Stankevich and His Moscow Circle* (1966), *Major Soviet Authors: Essays in Criticism* (1973), and *Mayakovsky: A Poet in the Revolution* (1973).

Donald Davie went to Stanford University as a Professor of English in 1969 after having taught at Dublin University, the University of California at Santa Barbara, Cambridge University, University of Essex, Grinnell College and the University of Southern California. He has published eight volumes of poetry and verse-translations of *The Poems of Doctor Zhivago*. His critical and scholarly publications include *Purity of Diction in English Verse* (1952), *Articulate Energy* (1957), *Ezra Pound: Poet as Sculptor* (1964), and *Thomas Hardy and British Poetry* (1972).

Peter Demetz came to the United States in 1952 from his native Prague where he had completed a doctorate at Charles University. He took a second doctorate at Yale University where he has remained on the faculty since 1956. Since 1962 he has been Professor of German and Comparative Literature. From 1963 to 1969 he was Chairman of Yale's Department of German. In addition to having received Guggenheim and Yale Morse fellowships, he was awarded the Golden Goethe Medal in Germany. His books include *René Rilkes Prager Jahre* (1953), *Marx, Engels, und die Dichter* (1959), and *Theodor Fontane* (1964). He has edited or co-edited *Twentieth Century Views: Brecht* (1961), *An Anthology of German Literature* (1967), and *Post-War German Literature* (1970).

René Girard has been on the faculty of Indiana University, Duke, Bryn Mawr, Johns Hopkins, where he was for eight years Chairman of the Department of Romance Languages, and State University of New York at Buffalo, where he was Faculty Professor of Arts and Letters and Distinguished Professor. In the Fall of 1974 he went to Stanford University as Professor of French, Comparative Literature, and Modern Thought. He has twice received Guggenheim fellowships. His books include *Mensonge romantique et vérité romanesque* (1961), *Marcel Proust: A Collection of Critical Essays* (1962), *Dostoevski: du double à l'unité* (1963), *Deceit, Desire and the Novel* (1967), and *La Violence et le Sacre* (1972).

Ihab Hassan came to the United States from his native Egypt in 1946. Following the completion of his doctorate at the University of Pennsylvania, he taught for two years at Rensselaer Polytechnic Institute before becoming a member of the faculty of Wesleyan University. At Wesleyan he was Benjamin L. Waite Professor of English from 1962 to 1970 and served at various times as Chairman of the English

Department, Director of the College of Letters, and Director of the Center for Humanities. Since 1970 he has been Vilas Research Professor at the University of Wisconsin (Milwaukee). His principal publications include *Radical Innocence: Studies in the Contemporary American Novel* (1961), *The Literature of Silence: Henry Miller and Samuel Beckett* (1967), *The Dismemberment of Orpheus: Toward a Post-Modern Literature* (1971), and *Contemporary American Literature, 1945-72* (1973).

Victor Lange studied at Oxford, the Sorbonne, the University of Munich, the University of Toronto, and the University of Leipzig, where he received his doctorate. Before joining the faculty of Princeton University in 1957 as a Professor of German, he had taught at Toronto and Cornell. Since 1968 he has been the John N. Woodhull Professor of Modern Languages at Princeton, and since 1962 an Honorary Professor of the Free University in Berlin. He has been a Guggenheim, McCosh, and NEH fellow, and in 1968-69 he was a Phi Beta Kappa Visiting Scholar. He is the author or editor of some two dozen books, among which one might mention *Modern German Literature* (1945), *Goethe's Fiction* (1953), *The Close of the Eighteenth Century* (1962), *Contemporary German Poetry* (1964), *The Reader in the Strategy of Fiction* (1972), and *The Age of Revolution* (1974).

Michael Riffaterre studied at the Sorbonne and received his doctorate at Columbia University, where he has been a member of the faculty since 1953. He has also been a visiting faculty member at Queens College and the University of Pennsylvania. Since 1955 he has served as Associate Editor of the *Romanic Review*. He received the Ansley Award from the Columbia University Press in 1955 and was a Guggenheim Fellow in 1961-62. Among his publications are *Le style des Pléiades de Gobineau* (1957), *Criteria for Style Analysis* (1959), and *Describing Poetic Structures* (1966).

Edward Wasiolek is the Avalon Professor of Comparative Literature and Russian at the University of Chicago. He has been Chairman of the Comparative Literature Program at Chicago since 1969 and of the Department of Slavic Languages and Literatures since 1971. Earlier he had taught English as a faculty member at Ohio Wesleyan and Chicago. He received the Quantrell Teaching Prize at the University of Chicago in 1961 and the Laing Press Prize in 1972. In addition to such books as *Crime and Punishment and the Critics* (1961), *Dostoevski: the Modern Fiction* (1964), and *The Brothers Karamozov and the Critics* (1967), he has edited for publication Dostoevski's notebooks for his four major novels and for *A Raw Youth.*

René Wellek received his Ph.D. from Charles University in Prague, and has since received honorary degrees from Lawrence College, Oxford, Harvard, Rome, University of Maryland, Boston College, Columbia, Montreal, Louvain, Michigan, and Munich. During his first seven years in this country he was a member of the faculty of Iowa University, and since 1946 has been associated with Yale, where as Professor of Slavic and Comparative Literature he served as Director of Comparative Literature, and Sterling Professor of Comparative Literature from 1952 to 1972. He is now Sterling Professor Emeritus. He has received virtually all of the major academic fellowships, including three Guggenheim fellowships. His major books include *Imannuel Kant in England* (1931), *The Rise of English Literary History* (1941), *Theory of Literature* (co-authored with Austin Warren) (1949), *Concepts of Criticism* (1963), *Confrontations* (1965), and *Discriminations* (1970). Since 1955 four volumes of his massive *A History of Modern Criticism* have appeared. He has held numerous editorships and offices in professional associations, including the Presidency both of the American Comparative Literature Association and of the International Comparative Literature Association.

INDEX

Index